2002

Confession and Community in the Novel

Confession and Community in the Novel

Terrence Doody

LOUISIANA STATE UNIVERSITY PRESS
Baton Rouge and London

Manufactured in the United States of America

Designer: Joanna Hill
Typeface: Linotype Palatino
Typesetter: Service Typesetters
Printer: Thomson-Shore, Inc.
Binder: John H. Dekker and Sons

Grateful acknowledgment is made for permission to use material that originally appeared as "The Underground Man's Confession and His Audience," in *Rice University Studies*, LXI (Winter, 1975), 27–38, and "Shreve McCannon and the Confessions of *Absalom, Absalom!*" in *Studies in the Novel*, VI (Winter, 1974), 454–69.

Library of Congress Cataloging in Publication Data

Doody, Terrence, 1943–
Confession and community in the novel.

Includes index.
1. Fiction—History and criticism. 2. Confession in literature. I. Title
PN3351.D66 823'.03 79–26388
ISBN 0–8071–0662–3

For Kathleen

May she be granted beauty and yet not . . .
Lose natural kindness and maybe
The heart-revealing intimacy
That chooses right

Contents

Acknowledgments

In a book that proposes community as an ultimate value, it is especially gratifying to be able to thank everyone who fostered it. So, I would like to thank first the Department of English of Rice University for its votes of confidence, and also Beverly Jarrett and Frank D. McConnell for their votes too. And I want to thank again for their loving understanding and kindness through hard times Eleanor Glass, Barry and Peggy Moore, Lynn Randolph, and Harry and Macey Reasoner. I am also grateful to Margaret Sloan.

As I was beginning to think about confessions, I was lucky to teach a course in autobiographical forms with Wes Morris, who taught me a great deal and whose ideas are everywhere throughout this essay. In various early stages, he read this manuscript, as did Dennis Huston and Walter Isle, and to all of them I am grateful for corrections, suggestions, and encouragement. As chairman, Walter Isle also cleared time for me to write. Bob Patten and Max Apple read the first full draft with great care and tact, and the changes they suggested were always for the better. But to each of them I owe an even greater thanks for their constant, generous, and truly inventive encouragement. I also owe a strong thanks to two unnamed readers whose suggestions grew into large and important improvements in the book. And I owe as much at least to Rose Graham, Sue Davis, and Pam Thompson for typing that has been fast, cheerful, and almost flawless in circumstances that have always been intense. I also owe thanks for many things to David Minter. For listening, reading, rereading, proofreading, and insisting on clarity, however, no one is due more than Macey Reasoner. And for everything, I owe Rachelle nothing less in return.

I

Confession and Its Audience

Chapter 1

Confession and Community

No one who is not interested in himself can be interested in a great novel.

JOHN BAYLEY
Tolstoy and the Novel

This is an essay on confession and on some of the ways confession can inform a novel. *The Confessions of St. Augustine* and *The Confessions of Jean-Jacques Rousseau* appear nonetheless in the pages of the second chapter because it is impossible to exclude them from any serious discussion of confessional narrative, and because they also illustrate the nature of confessional rhetoric. This essay, however, is not intended to be a history of the confession, and it is not an attempt to define the confessional novel. The affinities that the novel and the confession have—an essential interest in the experience of the individual, who lives in a material world, in time, and in relation to other people—give them a natural and illuminating perspective on each other; but the particular nature of confession gives the novels it informs a rhetorical attitude that is not simply common to all other first-person novels. "Confessions," as Stephen Spender says, "must always be made to confessors."[1] This means the reader of a written confession becomes a confessor, and the nature of his reading is thereby changed. What these changes are, the new expectations they create, the meaning all these give to a confessional statement, I explain through three novels: Daniel Defoe's *Moll Flanders*, Fyodor Dostoevsky's *Notes from Underground*, and Herman Melville's *Moby-Dick*.

These novels together show confession to be an essential element of novels that in every other way are quite different and to be the intention of first-person narrators who otherwise have little in common. The three do not exhaust the possibilities of confessional fiction and are not exhausted themselves by this confessional reading. In fact, each resists strict definition and actively questions its own premises or the expectations its premises seem to set up. This very resistance is an almost necessary result of the novel's interest in the experience of the individual. The individual's own interest in defining himself is one of the primary motives of confession. Randall Jarrell's definition of the novel as "a prose work of some length that has something wrong with it" is also a warning about definitions that are too prescriptive, exclusive, or reductive. And the spirit of this warning should apply to confessions as well. For although the confessions considered here are literary works, confession itself cannot be defined as merely a literary mode.

A confession is the deliberate, self-conscious attempt of an individual to explain his nature to the audience who represents the kind of community he needs to exist in and to confirm him. Confession is always an act of community, and the speaker's intention to realize himself in community is the formal purpose that distinguishes confession from other modes of autobiography or self-

1. Stephen Spender, *The Making of a Poem* (London: Hamish Hamilton, 1955), 71.

expression. This same formal purpose also distinguishes confessional novels from other first-person novels, which have different intentions and different attitudes toward their audience. For no one can make a confession without addressing a confessor, and no one would make a confession without a need for the confessor he addresses. But in no case is the confessor simply established, already there, as the representative of an existing social arrangement. Even Augustine, who addresses his confession directly to God, tries to create from his readers a community to hear and sustain him. His writing tells us something about confession and about the nature of the community it seeks, for in addition to God, his religious order, the episcopacy, and the communion of the Christian church, Augustine needed something more, which he embodies in the confessor he creates.

I use the term *confessor* to mean only the one who hears it, the speaker's audience. This usage amounts to more than a matter of convenience, for by using the term throughout this essay, I want to keep making the point that confession has a deliberate, formal intention which includes the confessor in the nature of the act. It seems necessary to emphasize terminology because *confession* is one of those literary terms that has been used to cover a multitude of sins. In much recent literary journalism, *confession* and *confessional* have come to mean both praise and blame of a writer's shamelessness or self-regard; they have been corrupted from terms of definition into value judgments. In more formal criticism, *confession* is often used quite broadly to include all kinds of autobiographical materials and intentions; and at least one school proposes that all literature can be read with the tools of psychoanalysis for its inadvertently confessional significance. This latter kind of criticism has its value; but it is the confessor's role and the speaker's active expectation of the confessor's response, rather than the nature of the speaker's themes or the unconscious intimacy of his self-revelation, that make community the most fitting, useful standard by which to consider and judge these confessional narratives.

For by community I mean something more than the solely

aesthetic relationship between the writer or narrator and his audience. Community is a moral relationship that implies mutual, personal responsibility. This relationship is not hard to understand in the confessions we receive in life, but it is not our usual way of perceiving the act of reading. Yet Moll Flanders does not merely want to be understood by her audience; she wants to be useful to the community she has entered, and expects to be granted the freedom and integrity warranted by her intention, in spite of the sensational story she tells. And Ishmael wants from his confessor not only confirmation that he is indeed now Ishmael, but also requital for the guilt he feels and the love he has lost in surviving Queequeg's death. The idea of community is something of an ideal whose exact meaning differs in each case I discuss, but it always involves the speaker's expectation that his deliberate self-definition will be answered with understanding, sympathy, and acceptance.

To see this formal expectation, however, we must not become distracted by subject matter—perhaps a strange thing to say of a genre that gives accounts of Rousseau's masturbation and Moll's adventures as a whore. Yet Robert Langbaum makes essentially the same point about the dramatic monologue, a form not unlike confession, which contains, among other things, the Duke of Ferrara's statement that he has murdered his last duchess. Langbaum says: "Form is a better index of tradition than subject matter in that subject matter is often controversial; it is often an index of what people think they believe, whereas form is an index of what is believed too implicitly to be discussed."[2] Langbaum's insight applies to more than tradition, and form is not so implicit that he cannot talk about it himself. To discuss the form confession gives to the novels before us and to understand what each of them proposes under the umbrella of community, we must look more carefully at the preliterary or extraliterary uses of confession, at the relation of those uses to psychoanalytic theory, and then at

2. Robert Langbaum, *The Poetry of Experience* (New York: W. W. Norton, 1963), 36.

that theory's relation to various theories of reading. A study of what is involved in reading a confession leads naturally to a discussion of community.

When we look beyond confessional narratives to the institutionalized modes confession itself has taken in our culture, we can see that a confession's formal intention, whatever its content, is always to win for the self the confirmation of a community. Institutional confessions are a part of both religious practice and legal procedure. A Christian penitent can examine his conscience in private, but he must confess to the priest or give witness before the congregation. In doing so, he defines himself according to the community's canons and confirms its authority; and by returning to the fold, he asks for the community's confirmation of himself. In *The Compulsion to Confess*, Theodor Reik says that confession is intrinsic to almost all religions and that "the admission of sins was, indeed, originally made to the community from which the sinner had been excluded, and it was considered the condition for his reentry. The image of the father in heaven that the penitent, as well as the one who prays, addresses, in his admission of sin, gives testimony to the fact that religious confession originated in the confession made to the earthly father."

The outlaw, who makes his confession to the proper authority, requests a similar embrace. By confessing, he accepts the civil or social norms that identify him as a criminal; for whatever reason, he wants to move back into the legal community and, therefore, accepts its right to censure him. Reik says: "In his confession, the criminal has admitted his misdeed to the community, as the child once admitted his naughtiness to his real father or to his substitute. As the confession of the child unconsciously represents a new wooing for love, an attempt at regaining the lost object, the criminal shows in his confession his intention to re-enter society by declaring himself deserving of punishment. The outsider is on his painful detour back to the family of man."[3]

3. Theodor Reik, *The Compulsion to Confess: On the Psychoanalysis of Crime and Punishment* (New York: Farrar, Straus and Cudahy, 1959), 304, 279. See also Erik Berggren, *The Psychology of Confession*, Studies in the

Throughout his book, Reik speaks of the various causes and effects of confession. He says, for instance: "By confession, we become acquainted with ourselves. It offers the best possibility of self-understanding and self-acceptance." And he is eloquent in describing any confessional speaker's "urge to re-conquer the lost love of the external world through the very confession." He is even almost witty in describing our natural avidity to hear a confession in every statement we attend. "In life we behave as we do in analysis, trusting the other person's unconscious compulsion to confess more than his conscious self-representation. In life, as in fiction, we feel intuitively or try to guess essential features of the unconscious character from the details of conscious self-characterization." Yet for Reik the essence of a confession is its unconscious compulsion. The analysand reveals himself in a code he does not fully understand. His analyst is a surrogate of the audience the speaker cannot address in person because of his guilt, which nonetheless compels him to confess "impulses and drives which are felt or recognized as forbidden."[4]

On the basis of a belief like Reik's, that the full truth of any expression resides only in the unconscious, it is possible to construct a theory of confession that holds all literature to be confessional in some degree. Reik, in fact, adumbrates such a theory when he says that "the representation of those inner processes of the persons in drama and the novel, may be an expression of . . . the effectiveness of the compulsion to confess."[5] From a completely different angle, in *The Nature of Narrative,* Robert Scholes and Robert Kellogg sketch a similar position—and also demonstrate how cavalierly the term *confession* has been used.

> One effect of modern empiricism has been to blur the distinction between the pure historical and mimetic

---

History of Religions, XXIX (Leiden: E. J. Brill, 1975). Berggren's book is especially interesting for its study of famous religious confessors, such as St. Francis of Sales.

4. Reik, *Compulsion to Confess,* 205, 222, 308–309, 195.

5. *Ibid.,* 307.

> forms of narrative on the one hand and the novel on the other. After the final, powerful impact of the autobiography, for example, on the novels of Proust, Joyce, Lawrence, Wolfe, and Fitzgerald—to mention only a few obvious instances—a clear distinction between the confession and the novel can no longer be sustained. The convergence of the novel with history, biography, and autobiography has resulted not so much from impatience with the story-teller's fantasy as from a modern skepticism of knowing anything about human affairs in an entirely objective (non-fictional) way. Science seems to have demonstrated that Aristotle's distinction between history and fiction was one of degree, not of kind. All knowing and all telling are subject to the conventions of art. Because we apprehend reality through culturally determined types, we can report the most particular event only in the form of a representational fiction, assigning motives, causes, and effects according to an absolute truth.[6]

So, using culturally determined types like those in psychoanalytic formulas, Frederick Crews can give a confessional reading of Hawthorne's works and Hawthorne himself in *The Sins of the Fathers*, as Norman N. Holland can give confessional interpretations of Matthew Arnold's "Dover Beach" and Federico Fellini's *La Dolce Vita* in *The Dynamics of Literary Response*.

Still, however valuable a theory like Reik's may be, however instructive Crews and Holland are, they do not accommodate the conscious intention involved in making a confession, nor do they respond to the experience of hearing a deliberately confessional statement. Whatever the displacement that figures in Reik's religious and legal models of confession—from the earthly father to the heavenly father, or from the parental authority to the social authority—there is also the conscious purpose of the criminal and penitent to define themselves in a way that allows their reentrance

6. Robert Scholes and Robert Kellogg, *The Nature of Narrative* (London: Oxford University Press, 1968), 151.

to a community. And we do not first listen to the voices of Augustine and Rousseau, or of Ishmael and Joseph Conrad's Marlow, in the way that Reik has listened to his patients or that Crews has analyzed Hawthorne after several rereadings. We observe Augustine and Rousseau as they present themselves in confessions written with a conscious purpose, great skill, and intense rhetoric. They define themselves as completely and advantageously as they can, with the expectation that their readers will pay close attention to the "details of conscious self-characterization," and with the equivalent confidence that their arts of persuasion will win for them acceptance on their own terms. The authority of their self-consciousness is as interesting as their need to talk about themselves in their way, and what this quality of intention asks of us as readers and confessors is what I examine here.

"An important part of our experience of almost any literary work is the sense that we are being talked to," Walter Slatoff says. "Our very decision that a group of words are worth attending to is in part a decision that the teller is worth listening to." Slatoff believes that literary criticism should acknowledge the act of reading, the act of a real reader who is not merely a phenomenological "consciousness" or a trained "competent"; and he says "that it is worth thinking about what happens when we do" read.[7] Slatoff's book, *With Respect to Readers,* is in many ways a response to Wayne C. Booth's *The Rhetoric of Fiction,* and it makes an objection to what I think of as Booth's "authoritarian optimism." In two central statements, Booth says:

> It is not, after all, only an image of himself that the author creates. Every stroke implying his second self will help to mold the reader into the kind of person suited

7. Walter J. Slatoff, *With Respect to Readers: Dimensions of Literary Response* (Ithaca, N.Y.: Cornell University Press, 1970), 93 and 3. The reader is a phenomenological consciousness in Wolfgang Iser, *The Implied Reader* (Baltimore: Johns Hopkins University Press, 1974), particularly the final chapter. For the reader as "competent," see Stanley E. Fish, *Self-Consuming Artifacts* (Berkeley: University of California Press, 1972), especially the Appendix.

> to appreciate such a character and the book he is writing.
>
> . . . .
>
> But the implied author of each novel is someone with whose beliefs on all subjects I must largely agree if I am to enjoy his work. Of course, the same distinction must be made between myself as reader and the often very different self who goes about paying bills, repairing leaky faucets, and failing in generosity and wisdom. It is only as I read that I become the self whose beliefs coincide with the author's. Regardless of my real beliefs and practices, I must subordinate my mind and heart to the book if I am to enjoy it to the full. The author creates, in short, an image of himself and another image of his reader; he makes his reader as he makes his second self, and the most successful reading is one in which the created selves, author and reader, can find complete agreement.[8]

Booth's formulations are essentially more aesthetic than critics who object to his moralism are willing to admit. He intends his formulas to apply to all sorts of novels with very different kinds of narrators, and he has developed a valuable method of analysis. But the union Booth defines between author and reader is not, to my mind, a conscious or even desirable experience for the reader. What Booth presents is an ideal of successful rhetoric and a rather sophisticated reader's acknowledgment that this is how an author may want his rhetoric to succeed. In the actual act of reading, as Slatoff insists, the reader never quite loses himself so successfully, and his reading involves less joy, less harmony and submission, and more conflict and contention than Booth wants to allow. Yet Booth's statements inadvertently suggest what a confessional speaker desires of his confessor, for they define the intensity a confession usually projects and the immediate need the speaker has for his confessor's confirmation. Still, in the best confessions we will read, the speaker does not ask the confessor to be his image, but his real equal. There is, in the relationship of com-

8. Wayne C. Booth, *The Rhetoric of Fiction* (Chicago: University of Chicago Press, 1961), 89, 137–138.

munity between them, a freedom that Booth does not acknowledge between narrator and reader; and in this freedom, the confessor's responsibility to the speaker is no greater than the speaker's responsibility to him.

Community itself is a rather vague word and difficult to define precisely because of its evolution. As Raymond Williams explains in *Keywords, community* has been used to mean both actual social groups and "a particular quality of relationship." By the nineteenth century, however, it was "the word normally chosen for experiments in an alternative kind of group-living," which implies for the group the desire for a particular quality of relationship unavailable elsewhere. And in the twentieth century, *community* has acquired what Williams calls a "polemical edge," with which it opposes the failures involved in contingencies of politics, nation, state. Williams says: "Community can be the warmly persuasive word to describe an existing set of relationships, or the warmly persuasive word to describe an alternative set of relationships. What is most important, perhaps, is that unlike all other terms of social organization . . . it seems never to be used unfavourably, and never to be given any positive opposing or distinguishing term."[9]

Community, as I use it, almost always means a positive alternative, a better quality of human relationships; as such, it is also something of an ideal to be achieved, for its opposing or distinguishing meaning is the particular state of isolation, dissatisfaction, discontinuity, or misunderstanding that the confessional speaker feels is the reason for making a confession. In defining himself, the speaker also defines his audience, and the state he expects them to share is the state of understanding that Ferdinand Toennies holds to be the heart of *Gemeinschaft*, his classical, technical term for what we call community. Toennies says: "Understanding is based upon intimate knowledge of each other in so far as this is conditioned and advanced by direct interest of one being in the life of the other, and readiness to take part in his joy and sorrow. For that reason understanding is the more probable,

9. Raymond Williams, *Keywords: A Vocabulary of Culture and Society* (New York: Oxford University Press, 1976), 65–66.

the more alike the constitution and experience or the more the natural disposition, character, and intellectual attitude are similar and harmonize."[10]

The direct interest in the life of another and a readiness to take part in his joy and sorrow is a moral state, an idea of community that adds to Booth's paradigm of implied author and implied reader the responsibility of the speaker to the confessor. Community is not simply achieved by the imposition of the speaker's identity and values on the audience, as it often seems to be in confessions like Rousseau's. Community is created between speaker and confessor out of mutual recognition, in the attempt to achieve a better quality of relationship.

Toennies also says: "The real organ of understanding, through which it develops and improves, is language. Language given by means of gestures and sounds enables expressions of pain and pleasure, fear and desire, and all other feelings and emotions to be imparted and understood. . . . It is itself the living understanding both in its content and form."[11] Toennies' faith in language may or may not be, in the context of literary criticism, a truism; but restating it is necessary because it is language that creates the understanding between a speaker and confessor who do not originally share a similar constitution or character. Language itself can be their experience in common and the source of their intellectual and moral harmony, their community.

Language is also the common ground of the confessions we hear from people we know, authors we read long dead, and fictional characters who live only in novels. Augustine and Rousseau both wrote to a living audience—Rousseau read portions of his *Confessions* aloud to various salons—but this is not an advantage either Ishmael or Marlow has. And in reading any of their confessions, we need not feel the enthusiastic responsibility Holden Caulfield feels in wanting to call the author on the phone. The

10. Ferdinand Toennies, *Gemeinschaft and Gesellschaft*, in Talcott Parsons *et al.* (eds.), *Theories of Society: Foundations of Modern Sociological Theory* (2 vols.; New York: Free Press of Glencoe, 1961), I, 196.

11. *Ibid.*

paradigm of confession I want to propose here concerns a particular kind of first-person narrative, or narrative act that is a way of talking about the self, which has toward its audience a specific intention. And I want to do this to call attention to these books and to ourselves as we read them, for they ask us to be not merely readers but confessors too, to enter an aesthetic relationship that has a moral character as well.

What the confessor then does with the confession—an equally important aspect of confession—I deal with in the second part of this essay. The confessor's response cannot *make* a confession, but it can make of an otherwise more guarded statement a confessional act—although not exactly in Reik's way of intuiting unconscious character from the details of the speaker's statement. What Reuben Jephson does with Clyde Griffiths' confession, what Nick Carraway does with Gatsby's, what Marlow does with Lord Jim's, and Quentin with Rosa's and Sutpen's, are all very different things. In *An American Tragedy, The Great Gatsby, Lord Jim,* and *Absalom, Absalom!,* however, the confessor is also a fully developed character; and two of these confessors, Marlow's privileged correspondent and Quentin's roommate, Shreve, are figures of the reader—not his surrogates, but models of his anticipated participation and possible response. Their presence as models affects the way we read these books and think of ourselves in their audience. Moreover, these four novels are a natural formal grouping; for they display to us, if we see them together, the variety and importance of the confessor's role, and they demonstrate the richness of the confessional act and its ramifications by their emphasis on the confessors' responsibility toward the speakers. The formal intention of confession does not change; it is always the deliberate attempt of a speaker to identify himself to a confessor who represents the community the speaker needs. But the ultimate meaning of a confession can be changed by its audience as it embraces or rejects the speaker. For this reason, the speaker must make his confessor as he makes his confession, because in no case before us is community simply a *donnée.*

Chapter 2

Confession's Rhetoric: Making a Confessor

Far from fearing death, I watched it coming joyfully. But I was reluctant to leave my fellow men before they had learnt my true worth, before they knew how deserving I should have appeared of their love if they had known me better.

JEAN-JACQUES ROUSSEAU
The Confessions of Jean-Jacques Rousseau

When you hear a man confessing, you know that he is not free.

AUGUSTINE
The Confessions of St. Augustine

From David Ogilvy's book *Confessions of an Advertising Man* we do not get exactly what we expect from the title, unless we think of the title as an oxymoron. We commonly expect literary confessions to be serious autobiographical statements that openly reveal private and often scandalous matters. But *Confessions of an Advertising Man* is not at all a confession; its title is a headline for Ogilvy's advertisement of his own success. One reason for his success is that Ogilvy clearly recognizes the appeal of the word *confessions* and uses it because of its rhetorical power.

Kenneth Burke says "the basic function of rhetoric" is "the use of words by human agents to form attitudes or to induce actions in other human agents." And he adds: "*It is rooted in an essential function of language itself, a function that is wholly realistic, and is continually born anew; the use of language as a symbolic means of inducing cooperation in beings that by nature respond to symbols."*[1] The cooperation that Ogilvy induces by the rhetoric of his title is the purchase of his book, which is still selling in paperback sixteen years after its publication in 1964. Burke's conception of rhetoric implies the use confession naturally makes of rhetoric in seeking the cooperation that defines community. Ideally, rhetoric should be unnecessary in talking to oneself, in fantasies, in keeping a journal or diary, in prayer; practically, however, we use rhetoric in these acts because rhetoric is also a means of creating and enacting a role. If the role we enact in confession is that of the outsider who seeks to enter a community, the rhetoric of confession will also attempt to induce the cooperation of the confessor in forming that community.

We overlook this rhetorical aspect of confession because our immediate appetite is for information rather than form, and so we think of confessions in terms of their normal themes of guilt, estrangement, or discontinuity. We also regard self-expression so highly, we have come to think of it as self-fulfilling, its own end. Burke's sense of rhetoric, however, allows him to see beneath its disguises and transformations, and what he says in the following paragraph explains not only why we overlook rhetoric, but also why it operates in confessions so essentially.

> Did you ever do a friend an injury by accident, in all poetic simplicity? Then conceive of this same injury as done by sly design, and you are forthwith within the orbit of Rhetoric. If you, like the Stendhals and Gides, conceive a character by such sophistication, Rhetoric as the speaker's attempt to identify himself favorably with his audience then becomes so transformed that the work may seem to have been written under an esthetic of pure "expression," without regard for communicative

1. Kenneth Burke, *A Rhetoric of Motives* (Berkeley: University of California Press, 1969), 41, 43.

> appeal. Or it may appeal perversely, to warped motives within the audience. Or it may be but an internalizing of the rhetorical motive, as the very actions of such a representative figure take on a rhetorical cast. Hence, having woven a rhetorical motive so integrally into the very essence of his conception, the writer can seem to have ignored rhetorical considerations; yet, in the sheer effrontery of his protagonist there is embedded, however disguised or transformed, an *anguish* of communication (communication being, as we have said, a generalized form of love).[2]

Love is the highest name we can give to community, and in confession especially there is "an *anguish* of communication." Critics have mostly defined confession under "an esthetic of pure 'expression' " and see its goal as catharsis or integration rather than as the realization of the self in community. Their definitions, however, are very helpful because they address the personal motives for making a confession, rather than the formal motive, and their discussions shift our attention to concrete examples.

In *Anatomy of Criticism*, Northrop Frye uses the term *confession* in its broadest sense to designate almost all autobiographical writing. Frye says confession is "introverted, but intellectualized in content and inspired by a creative, and therefore fictional, impulse to select only those events and experiences in the writer's life that go to build up an integrated pattern. This pattern may be something larger than himself with which he has come to identify himself or simply the coherence of his character and attitudes." Frye goes on to say: "Nearly always some theoretical and intellectual interest in religion, politics, or art plays a leading role in the confession. It is his success in integrating his mind on such subjects that makes the author feel that his life is worth writing about." Frye sees no "literary reason why the subject of a confession should always be the author himself," as in the case of *Moll Flanders*, and he links the confession to other forms of fiction-

2. *Ibid.*, 37.

alized autobiography.[3] Frye's emphasis on intention and integration is appropriate to confession more strictly defined, but his necessary level of generalization is finally misleading because his sense of an autobiography's success is not quite appropriate to confession.

In *The Modern Confessional Novel*, Peter M. Axthelm's field of inquiry is narrower than Frye's, and his conclusions are less sanguine. Axthelm does not find that it is the speaker's "success in integrating his mind" that provides the impulse to confess. "The confessional novel presents a hero, at some point in his life, examining his past as well as his innermost thoughts, in an effort to achieve some sort of perception." This notion of perception is somewhat vague; but as he elaborates this description, Axthelm argues that the confessional speaker is "afflicted and unbalanced, disillusioned and groping for meaning." The speaker does not always, or even usually, have something "larger than himself" to identify with; the "integrated pattern" of his life or the "coherence of his character and attitudes" is more often the end he hopes to discover rather than the premise from which he can begin. Axthelm strongly implies that a confession proceeds from a crisis, that the need to confess is itself critical.[4] This insight advances our understanding of confession beyond Frye's formula; but, for Axthelm, the confessional audience is only incidental to the essential act, and he makes very little distinction between a confession made very explicitly to an audience—*Notes from Underground*—and one made to no audience at all—*Herzog*. Axthelm calls *Herzog* a confession, although it is not even a first-person narrative.

In his study of modern confessional poetry, Robert Phillips defines confession, in effect, by listing sixteen characteristics of the confessional style. Phillips stresses the poet's pain, imbalance, dislocation, failure, his courage in speaking out, and his need for a therapeutic purgation. Phillips moves even farther away from Frye than Axthelm does when he points out that madness is often

3. Northrop Frye, *Anatomy of Criticism* (Princeton, N.J.: Princeton University Press, 1957), 307, 308.

4. Peter M. Axthelm, *The Modern Confessional Novel* (New Haven, Conn.: Yale University Press, 1967), 8ff.

the motive or the subject of many confessional poems. Like Axthelm, he sees the confession as a search for integration and wholeness rather than as a demonstration of them. Phillips also recognizes the confession's necessary openness to its audience: "There are no barriers between the reader and the poet."[5] Still, he is more interested in themes than in form; the openness between the reader and the poet bespeaks the poet's candor, not his formal intention. When he cites *The Prelude* as an important antecedent of modern confessional poems, Phillips does not mention that Wordsworth addresses his poem to Coleridge, which makes *The Prelude* specifically confessional and acknowledges the confessional tradition from which it grew.[6]

Francis R. Hart approaches confession in a completely different way, by distinguishing it from apology and memoir. His definition is the most abstract, but it is also the richest because it is the most formalistic. Hart, moreover, recognizes the audience's importance to the form.

> "Confession" is personal history that seeks to communicate or express the essential nature, the truth, of the self. "Apology" is personal history that seeks to demonstrate or realize the integrity of the self. "Memoir" is personal history that seeks to articulate or repossess the historicity of the self. "Confession" as an impulse or intention places the self relative to nature, reality; "apology" places the self relative to social and/or moral law; "memoir" places the self relative to time, history, cultural pattern, and change. Confession is ontological; apology ethical; memoir historical and cultural. As these or any comparable definitions suggest, such intentions must overlap; one can hardly appear in total independence of the others. In practice, they complement or succeed or conflict with each other. Every autobiography

5. Robert Phillips, *The Confessional Poets* (Carbondale: Southern Illinois University Press, 1973). See Chap. 1, especially 16–17.

6. See Frank D. McConnell, *The Confessional Imagination: A Reading of Wordsworth's Prelude* (Baltimore: Johns Hopkins University Press, 1974), Chap. 1.

> can appropriately and usefully be viewed as in some degree a drama of intention, and its dramatic intentionality is another component of the autobiographical situation for the interpreter to attend to.[7]

So, while a confession is a definition of the ontological self, it must also be an apology for the self, a realization of the self in social or ethical terms; and this necessary apologetic element in every confession is what, in Hart's scheme, admits the audience to the confessional. Hart finds in Rousseau the most significant example of the way in which this kind of apology works. Calling Rousseau's *Confessions* a confession and an apology both, he identifies Rousseau's "characteristic act of friendship, an apology . . . intended to achieve at last the society his life consistently failed to achieve."[8] Stephen Spender makes much the same point. "The essence of confession is that the one who feels outcast pleads with humanity to relate his isolation to its wholeness. He pleads to be forgiven, condoned, condemned even, so long as he is brought back into the wholeness of people and of things."[9]

Spender's formula, like Theodor Reik's, defines the general motive of confession as guilt alone, and therefore it also extends the definition of the confessor to "the wholeness of people and things," as Reik speaks of "the family of man." As we have seen, the confessions of penitents and criminals do proceed from guilt, and outlaws from Moll Flanders to Felix Krull have long been the subjects of confessional novels. Even these criminals, however, do not talk only about their crimes; in their full-scale explanations of themselves, they also talk about their nature, their identity. However real their crimes may be, their outlawry is also a symbolic state or metaphor for their estrangement from a community. Ishmael takes the name *Ishmael* to begin his confession, in which he does not admit to any crimes but does try to tell us who he is.

7. Francis R. Hart, "Notes for an Anatomy of Modern Autobiography," *New Literary History*, I (Spring, 1970), 491–92.

8. *Ibid.*, 508.

9. Stephen Spender, *The Making of a Poem* (London: Hamish Hamilton, 1955), 69.

His confession is a better general model than a criminal's because it also makes the point that a confession can be made to an audience that does not represent the whole of humanity but does embody a particular community in which the speaker seeks a quality of relationship beyond mere forgiveness.

Raskolnikov's two confessions in *Crime and Punishment* only appear to fill Spender's prescription, but in both of them he is concerned with more than his crime and guilt. Raskolnikov has murdered the old pawnbroker to prove himself an extraordinary man, one who is beyond the law. In committing a perfect, undetected crime, however, he cannot prove this. He must confess to the police magistrate Porfiry Petrovich, who has admired his ideas, in order to be recognized by the legal community he has violated. Raskolnikov can tell Porfiry Petrovich what he has done and why; but he also confesses to Sonya Marmaledov in order to explain to her, and to himself, who he is—as Sonya's father has tried to explain to Raskolnikov who *he* is. Raskolnikov chooses Sonya specifically because she too is an outcast and, unlike Porfiry Petrovich, understands the need and function of suffering. She can embrace him in a community informed by an eternal rather than temporal law, and what she offers to him, in a way that Porfiry Petrovich cannot, is the recognition that he needs to understand himself and the pain that has pushed him toward madness. Porfiry Petrovich can ratify the implications of Raskolnikov's intellectual ambitions; Sonya can recognize his need for love in a new order. Her importance as his confessor is signaled by the fact that Raskolnikov cannot make his confession either to his sister Dunya or to Razumikhin. They love him deeply, but they have not undergone the suffering he and Sonya have, and they represent the fatherless community Raskolnikov has tried to transcend. Sonya sees in Raskolnikov the same need for renewal she sees in herself.

Raskolnikov's confessions are illustrative but not wholly typical. Every confession is an act of individuation. And most of the confessions in literature and in life come from an individual who must confess himself, not because he has done anything wrong, but simply because he no longer understands himself fully and has to talk himself out. His confession is a personal history, a deliberate and self-conscious act of self-definition, by which he tries to explain the reality of his life in order to give it a conscious integrity and continuity. His confession issues from a personal crisis; and in most cases, making a confession is his attempt to resolve that crisis. (In some cases, like Moll Flanders', the crisis has been resolved in time, and the confession is the speaker's attempt to explain the meaning of that resolution and extend it.) In every case, however, the speaker confesses to an audience who represents the community he needs to exist in and confirm his identity. His need for community is intrinsic to his personal motive for making a confession; and though he does want to be brought back into "the human family" and into "the wholeness of people and things," his confession itself defines that wholeness according to his own needs and desires, which he embodies in the confessor he creates.

He must create the confessor because he usually feels that no available institution, no system or myth, no class structure, profession, locale, or family quite accommodates his full sense of his individuality. His confession expresses his sense of disconnection between what he should be, or appears to be, and what he really is. What the individual appears to be is often the ensemble of his public attributes—his conventional role, his profession, his status—the significance of which is not irrelevant to his sense of his full identity, though it defines only his ethical self. His full identity involves, to use Hart's word, his ontological self as well, which is a more basic, personal, comprehensive, and undetermined reality. This ontological aspect of identity is internal and continuous, however mutable it seems, and it includes the sense of the self that is expressed in predilections, style, memories, dreams, and aspirations; in our relationships with those we love and need; in the usually troubled conviction that *this* is who I am, regardless.[10] It is this sense of identity that Roy Pascal points to when he says of

10. This sense of identity is derived from Erik H. Erikson, *Identity, Youth, and Crisis* (New York: W. W. Norton, 1968). See Prologue, especially 22–23.

every autobiographer: "He exists for himself as something uncompleted, something full of potentiality, always overflowing the actuality, and it is this indeterminateness and unlimitedness that he communicates to us as an essential quality of his being."[11]

Lord Jim's confession to Marlow is as good an example of this kind of confession as Raskolnikov's to Sonya. Jim is guilty. He does not, however, expect the maritime court to understand him. He stays, testifies, and accepts the court's verdict, but he must make another confession to Marlow, in the Malabar House, to explain that he is not fully defined by either the cowardice he has shown or the court's official opinion of him. His choice of Marlow as his confessor, however accidental at first, is crucial: what if he had tried to talk to Brierly or Chester? Gatsby's choice of Nick Carraway is equally crucial. Gatsby does not expect the people of Long Island society to understand him; they are, Nick says, people who have paid Gatsby "the subtle tribute of knowing nothing whatever about him." Yet Gatsby, like Raskolnikov and Jim, wants recognition. When Daisy leaves him to return to Tom after the accident, Gatsby confesses to Nick, not his criminal activities, but that he is really James Gatz, who has tried to realize the dream of being someone else.

Neither Jim nor Gatsby "pleads with humanity," as Spender would have it, for neither thinks of himself in such broad terms. Each simply tries to explain himself, and each one receives the courage to make his confession from his needs and from the hope that the confessor will respond from his own need for sympathy, understanding, and community. Confession is always an act of intimacy, and it relies on the power intimacy itself can have to create a response. "It is certain my conviction gains infinitely, the moment another soul will believe in it," says Novalis, in the line Conrad uses as the epigraph to *Lord Jim*. Novalis' romantic confidence is undercut, however, by the process of confession itself, as *Lord Jim* demonstrates. Not just anyone will do as confessor. In confessing his identity, the speaker defines the confessor too,

11. Roy Pascal, *Design and Truth in Autobiography* (Cambridge, Mass.: Harvard University Press, 1960), 18.

defines the kind of community he needs. For the simply criminal, there is little problem: the authorities are there and the law is on the books. The penitent has a wider choice of congregations; if his choice does not literally create the community he chooses, his choice confirms that community. For the individual confessing his identity, the problem is more complex. The definition of his confessor involves the whole definition of himself. As he explains himself, he virtually instructs his confessional audience on how it should respond to him; and this response, in effect, becomes the confessor, the audience, the community he needs. Even Augustine, who makes his confession to God, defines the human community he needs to accept him.

Augustine confesses in order to understand himself in the eyes of God, to express his guilt and contrition as a sinner, and to comprehend the continuity of his life—"what now I am" and "what once I was"—which was so completely altered by his conversion.[12] In addressing his *Confessions* directly to God, Augustine commits himself to "absolute veracity; how could he falsify or dissimulate anything before One who can see into his innermost marrow?"[13] Augustine himself says to his omniscient God: "No one who makes a confession to you teaches you what takes place within him," and, "Lord, before whose eyes the abyss of man's conscience lies naked, what thing within me could be hidden from you, even if I would not confess it to you? I would be hiding you from myself, not myself from you."[14] The implication is that Augustine would also be hiding from himself and, therefore, would be isolated. This kind of prayer is Augustine's mode of apology, his ethical connection to something outside himself. And because he commits himself to God's judgment, he commits himself to an absolute self-knowledge. This discovery of what his own ontology

12. *The Confessions of St. Augustine*, trans. John K. Ryan (Garden City, N.Y.: Doubleday, 1960), X, iii, 4.

13. Jean Starobinski, "The Style of Autobiography," in Seymour Chatman (ed.), *Literary Style: A Symposium* (London: Oxford University Press, 1971), 289.

14. *Confessions of St. Augustine*, V, i, 1; X, ii, 2.

is in God's eyes is one of Augustine's means to salvation. But, of course, Augustine knows that he cannot share his confessor's omniscience, that his self-knowledge will always be incomplete and "restless." He utters his most famous prayer on the first page of his *Confessions*: "For you have made us for yourself, and our heart is restless until it rests in you." This prayer is his expression of the kind of final community he needs—union with God.

Until this union is achieved, however, Augustine needs the human community he addresses in publishing his *Confessions*. He began the work in 397, ten years after his baptism, when he was the Bishop of Hippo, a famous and influential convert, and deeply engaged in a controversy over the nature of the Christian community. This controversy may have had an effect on the personal crisis he was also undergoing at the time, for it too involved the nature of community. Augustine was troubled some by the advent of middle age; he was also troubled by the persistent temptations created by his need for fame and by his strong concupiscence. He was troubled most, however, by the equanimity of some of his closest associates, men who did not share his restlessness. Throughout his life Augustine had a need for friends that was as great as his talent for making them. Even before his conversion, he had experimented with living in small communities that had the character of a monastic order; and he was attached to a group that called themselves *servi Dei*, ascetic lay intellectuals who had experienced a conversion like his own in the course of successful secular careers. However, many of these *servi Dei* had grown to feel about their conversions a "final certainty," a smugness Augustine did not have.[15] At least part of his motive in making a confession lay in his need to open himself to these associates and explain his own uncertainties, in order to disabuse them of their complacency, draw them closer to him, and win from them the understanding, confirmation, and prayers he needed as his daily bread.

15. Peter Brown, *Augustine of Hippo: A Biography* (Berkeley: University of California Press, 1969), 177. Brown is the source of all biographical information not contained in the *Confessions*.

In the tenth book of the *Confessions,* Augustine defines the human community he needs, the confessor he addresses through God. His definition is very careful, even torturous, for he is a bishop and teacher and is insistent about his primary purpose and method. He wants to affirm always the greater value of God's audience and to condemn mere human curiosity. He also wants to defend himself against skepticism by explaining that his own credibility and the utility of his *Confessions* are guaranteed by the charity that informs his proper human audience. He wants to define exactly not only that audience but also those he is *not* talking to. This definition of a possible antagonist is a rhetorical strategy common to many confessions; but it is also much more than merely a rhetorical strategy, for repudiating the unsympathetic is part of a confession's essential end.

> What have I to do with men, that they should hear my confessions as if they were to "heal all my diseases?" A race eager to know about another man's life, but slothful to correct their own! Why do they seek to hear from me what I am, men who do not want to hear from you what they themselves are? When they hear me speak about myself, how do they know if I speak the truth, since none among men know "what goes on with a man but the spirit of man which is in him?" But if they should hear about themselves from you, they cannot say, "The Lord lies!" What else is for them to hear from you about themselves except to know themselves? Who knows anything and yet says, "It is false," unless he is a liar? But because "charity believes all things" among them whom it unites by binding them to itself, I too, O Lord, will confess to you in such manner that men may hear, although I cannot prove to them that I confess truly. But those men whose ears charity opens to me believe me.[16]

Augustine constantly insists on the limitations of his human audience, and on his own, by asking the rhetorical questions only

16. *Confessions of St. Augustine,* X, iii, 3.

God can answer. He can hardly admit to the benefits of human community until he makes it clear that he belongs to God first and acts only as his instrument. But in making himself open and useful to other men through God, Augustine is also trying to apologize for his fame, the pride fame naturally brings, and his own need to be known. We can see in him the desire for humility that proud men must have to be holy.

> With what fruit then, O my Lord, to whom my conscience each day makes confession—more secure in its hope of your mercy than from any innocence of its own—with what fruit, I ask, do I confess, not only in your presence but to men also by these writings, what now I am, not what once I was? That other advantage I have seen and spoken of. But as to what I am now, at this very time when I make my confessions, many men wish to know about this, both men who have known me and others who have not known me. They have heard something from me or about me, but their ear is not placed close to my heart, where I am whatever I am. Therefore, they wish to hear me confess what I am within myself, where they can extend neither eye nor ear nor mind. This they desire, as men ready to believe; how otherwise could they know it? Charity, by reason of which they are good men, tells them that I do not lie when I make my confession: it is charity in them that believes in me.[17]

Though Augustine defines charity here as something more than *filia*, he explains its personal effect when he admits to the benefits charity's community can provide for him, to what his human audience can do for him by loving him for himself.

> But with what benefit do they wish to hear me? Do they wish to share my thanksgiving, when they hear how close it is by your gift that I approach to you, and to pray for me, when they hear how I am held back by my own weight? To such men will I reveal myself. It

17. *Ibid.*, X, iii, 4.

> is no small benefit, O Lord my God, that "thanks may be given to you by many in our behalf," and that many should pray to you for us. Let a brother's mind love in me what you teach us must be loved, and lament in me what you teach us must be lamented. Let a brother's mind do this, not a stranger's mind, not the mind "of strange children, whose mouth has spoken vanity, and their right hand is the right hand of iniquity." Let it be that brotherly mind which, when it approves me, rejoices over me, and when it disapproves of me, is saddened over me, for that reason that, whether it approves or disapproves, it loves me.[18]

Augustine's care in stating his needs in their proper hierarchical order—God's acceptance first, then the realization of his own vocation, and only then man's communal embrace—does not diminish the force of his need for community. His scrupulous discrimination and his eagerness to accept correction if it comes with love display his vulnerability and make his strength more poignant. For although he is fully aware of the human community's limitations, he can be enthusiastic about its solace and joys. In publishing the *Confessions*, he acknowledges that community itself is necessary for growth and happiness; and earlier in the text he has described at least one community in which he was happy.

> There were other things done in their company which more completely seized my mind: to talk and to laugh with them; to do friendly acts of service for one another: to read well-written books together; sometimes to tell jokes and sometimes to be serious; to disagree at times, but without hard feelings, just as a man does with himself; and to keep our many discussions pleasant by the very rarity of such differences; to teach things to others and to learn from them; to long impatiently for those who were absent, and to rejoice with joy those joining us. These and similar expressions, proceeding

18. *Ibid.*, X, iv, 5.

> from the hearts of those who loved and repaid their comrades' love, by way of countenance, tongue, eyes, and a thousand pleasing gestures, were like fuel to set our minds ablaze and to make but one of many.[19]

There is in this passage an erotic appreciation of community, and Augustine's Platonic tendency to make "but one of many" suggests the kind of integration that is possible for the individual whose community fosters serious acceptance, stimulation, variety, fraternal correction, intimacy, and love. These qualities are not necessarily inherent in a formal community like a congregation or an episcopacy; they are not guaranteed by faith and humility; they do not issue from self-knowledge. They are the properties of the kind of community Augustine needs for himself.

Northrop Frye says that Augustine "appears to have invented" the confession and that Rousseau "established a modern type of it."[20] It is probably more than coincidence that the two men have so much in common. Both were young men from the provinces—Hippo and Geneva—ambitious seminal thinkers, and powerful rhetoricians. Both, moreover, lived through and helped to define periods of major historical transition, when an exact definition of the self became valuable to an entire culture. Augustine lived through the fall of Rome and the great age of Christian heresy; Rousseau through the Enlightenment that fostered the French Revolution and the ages of democracy and romanticism. Yet their differences are important, too. Rousseau may be the first modern man; he is certainly an early model of the self-absorption, dislocations, and febrility that characterize the modern temperament. And he does not have the advantage of Augustine's faith in a personal God, nor does he have the kind of office Augustine had. In every sense, Rousseau is on his own. He briefly addresses a "Sovereign Judge" and "Eternal Being," but he is much more interested in his own sense of himself and in his readers' approbation. As

19. *Ibid.*, IV, viii, 13.
20. Frye, *Anatomy of Criticism*, 307.

Robert J. Ellrich says, Rousseau's "*Confessions* proclaim: I am *my* self."[21] Rousseau also asks that his readers relinquish themselves and their responses entirely to his direction.

Rousseau's *Confessions* grow out of a crisis that was lifelong: his dependency and need for love and his equal need for a fully independent self-possession.[22] He says of his childhood, and this is true of the rest of his life: "My strongest desire was to be loved by everyone who came near me," to be "idolized by everyone around me" and "always treated as a beloved son."[23] He later says, "Where happiness and enjoyment were concerned, I needed all or nothing."[24] All or nothing was what he demanded of life, of love and freedom, of his friends and readers. The terrible psychological conflict that ultimately inspired his *Confessions* is manifest in his reaction to winning the Dijon essay contest with the tract that became his *First Discourse.* Rousseau took the unexpected, independent position that the arts and sciences have not contributed to man's progress. His victory made him famous; his fame gave him the notion to retreat from society, in which he was awkward and inarticulate anyhow, so that he could live according to the "principle" of his own nature. Accepted, he had to become independent in order to be himself and to define exactly the grounds on which he wanted to be accepted.

In the *Confessions* Rousseau casts his ontological identity as that "principle" within him that has produced all his soul's "movements." He assumes that he is integrated and continuous and that he and his life are easily justifiable; for whatever contradictions

21. Robert J. Ellrich, *Rousseau and His Reader: The Rhetorical Situation of the Major Works,* University of North Carolina Studies in the Romance Languages and Literature, No. 83 (Chapel Hill: University of North Carolina Press, 1969), 81.

22. This dependency complex is one of the major themes of Lester G. Crocker's *Jean-Jacques Rousseau: The Quest (1712–1758)* (New York: Macmillan, 1968), I, and *Jean-Jacques Rousseau: The Prophetic Voice (1758–1778)* (New York: Macmillan, 1973), II.

23. *The Confessions of Jean-Jacques Rousseau,* trans. J. M. Cohen (Harmondsworth, England: Penguin Books, 1953), 25, 21.

24. *Ibid.,* 393.

he may contain and celebrate, it is always external circumstances and other people that are to blame for his life's troubles and disintegration.

> There is a certain sequence of impressions and ideas which modify those that follow them, and it is necessary to know the original set before passing any judgements. I endeavor in all cases to explain prime causes, in order to convey the interrelation of results. I should like in some way to make my soul transparent to the reader's eye, and for that purpose I am trying to present it from all points of view, to show it in all lights, and to contrive that none of its movements shall escape his notice, so that he may judge for himself of the principle which has produced them.
>
> . . . .
>
> It was not so much my literary celebrity as the change in my character, which dates from this time [winning the Dijon prize], that evoked their jealousy; they would perhaps have forgiven me for brilliance in the act of writing; but they could not forgive me for setting up an example by my conduct; this appeared to put them out. I was born for friendship; my easy and gentle disposition had no difficulty in fostering it. So long as I lived unknown to the public, I was loved by all who knew me, and had not a single enemy. But as soon as I made a name I ceased to have friends. That was a great misfortune. A still greater one was that I was surrounded by people who took the name of friend and used the rights it gave them only to drag me to my undoing.[25]

These two passages contain the essence of Rousseau's self-confidence and paranoia, his insight and blindness, his confessional impulse and his need to apologize constantly. His strong belief in his integrity and his great desire to be seen wholly, compel Rousseau to define his audience in terms of its perfect, unquestioning,

25. *Ibid.*, 169, 338.

undemanding acceptance of his version of himself. We must not merely take the name of friend; we have to identify with him and judge him not at all. His friends so-called are the whipping boys he uses, as Augustine uses the "strange children, whose mouth has spoken vanity," to define and repudiate those he is not talking to. Rousseau's real audience, his true confessors, will prove themselves also "born for friendship . . . easy and gentle." They will never violate him by having an opinion of his conduct that is not also *his*, and in the *Confessions* this conduct is not what Rousseau does, it is what he says he does. His demands on his audience are infantile and totalitarian—as though he were history's only child—and his words about himself are never more revealing than in the passage in which he explains the fate of his own five children.

In Book 8 of his *Confessions*, as he recounts his decision to withdraw from society, Rousseau also explains that his children were given away to orphanages in their infancy. He had told several people of this, but he was outraged that they told anyone else. He expects his reader to be sympathetic to the case he makes and to accept his contention that child abandonment is a less serious sin than judging him adversely for having committed it.

> It could never have been disclosed except by those in whom I had confided, and indeed it was not until after my break with them that it became public. By that fact alone they are judged. Without wishing to disown the blame which I deserve, I would rather have that on my conscience than have to answer, like them, for sheer maliciousness. My fault is great, but it was an error; I neglected my duties, but the desire to do harm never entered my head, and a father's feelings cannot speak very loudly for children he has never seen. But to betray a friend's confidence, to violate the most sacred of all bonds, to publish secrets entrusted to our bosom, deliberately to dishonor the friends we have deceived and who still respect us as they say good-bye—those are not faults; they are utter baseness and infamy.
>
> I have promised to write my confessions, but not to

> make my apologies; so I will stop here. My duty is to tell the truth; my readers' to be just, and that is all I shall ever ask of them.[26]

This statement, from the author of *Emile,* makes several clear points. First, "by that fact alone they are judged" involves a sense of criteria that Rousseau would never accept as applicable to himself. Second, "the most sacred of all bonds" is not paternity but Rousseau's confidence in those to whom he confesses. Third, the reader must uphold the imperatives of this confidence or be guilty himself of "utter baseness and infamy." Rousseau does not ask his readers to be just, he asks them to be unequivocally submissive. In doing so, he projects his own dependency onto them. They are free to think only as he tells them to; he is free only when someone else confirms his freedom.

The result of trying to create a sympathetic confessor who is given so little autonomy is that there is no way Rousseau can stop confessing, no place at which he can come to rest except in himself. Augustine ends the narrative portion of his *Confessions* with the death of his mother, Monica. In the ensuing books, he enacts his profession of faith and his vocation as a teacher by writing the theology, philosophy, and exegesis that make up his theories of memory, time, matter and form, and creation. Rousseau's only profession is himself. Throughout the final parts of his *Confessions,* he keeps promising a sequel. The *Confessions* as we have them now end with a very disturbing image of the kind of community he finally seeks—an audience bullied into silence, incapable of demurral.

> I have told the truth. If anyone knows anything contrary to what I have recorded, though he prove it a thousand times, his knowledge is a lie and an imposture; and if he refuses to investigate and inquire into it during my lifetime he is no lover of justice or of truth. For my part, I publicly and fearlessly declare that anyone, even if he has not read my writings, who will

26. *Ibid.,* 334–35.

> examine my nature, my character, my morals, my likings, my pleasures and my habits with his own eyes and can still believe me a dishonorable man, is a man who deserves to be stifled.
>
> Thus I concluded my reading, and everyone was silent. Mme. D'Egmont was the only person who seemed moved. She trembled visibly but quickly controlled herself, and remained quiet, as did the rest of the company. Such was the advantage I derived from my reading and declaration.[27]

Rousseau wanted to be taken, literally, at his word. He wrote his *Confessions* and then read them aloud, to salons like Mme. d'Egmont's, in sessions that lasted up to seventeen hours.[28] Whether Mme. d'Egmont was moved by sympathy or fear or the sheer spectacle is a question Rousseau does not answer in the ambiguity of the phrase "such was the advantage." It is an advantage that seems like conquest, a demonstration of his own integrity that results in isolation. Kenneth Burke says, "Persuasion involves choice, will; it is directed to a man only insofar as he is *free.*"[29] Yet, Rousseau would persuade his audience to relinquish its freedom to him in order to become, not the community of "comrades" in which Augustine could "make but one of many," but the creatures of Rousseau's own reverie.

At the outset of his confession in *The Immoralist*, André Gide's narrator Michel says: "That is all the help I need: to speak to you. For I am at a moment in my life past which I can no longer see my way. Yet this is not exhaustion. The point is I can no longer understand. I need . . . I need to speak, I tell you. The capacity to get free is nothing; the capacity to be free, that is the task."[30] Michel's words make perhaps the most succinct statement of the desire for self-renewal that every confession contains; they also

27. *Ibid.*, 605–606.
28. Crocker, II, 327.
29. Burke, *A Rhetoric of Motives*, 50.
30. André Gide, *The Immoralist*, trans. Richard Howard (New York: Random House, 1970), 7.

make a good description of the kind of freedom a confessional speaker seeks in a community that will confirm him and sustain his freedom. So, because it is an act of self-renewal and does seek his freedom, confession tends to be open-ended. As all autobiographical narrative must, confession articulates the speaker's historicity, but it does so in order to prepare for the future. An autobiography like Goethe's or an autobiographical novel like Joyce's *A Portrait of the Artist as a Young Man* can terminate somewhere in the author's past, but a confession must be made right up to the present for the sake of what lies beyond, in the community the confessional speaker creates. For this reason, confessions are often difficult to end, and their endings can be used as a measure of the speaker's confidence in himself and in his audience. Augustine obviously has more of this confidence than Rousseau has; and as we will see, Moll Flanders has more of it than the Underground Man.

Another measure of the speaker's sense of himself, his distance on himself and from his audience, is the quality of his rhetoric. However quietly he can define his own being, he must raise his voice to justify himself as he asks for acceptance. By means of his rhetoric, he can cast himself in any role he wants—usually the role of his authentic self—and make his apology to his confessor. So, rhetoric is more than persuasion; it is the social or ethical level of the speaker's voice, the tone he takes in community. And from this premise, we can draw a rule of thumb: the more sure of himself the speaker is, the closer he feels to himself, the less "rhetorical" his confession will be; the less a speaker trusts himself and his audience, the more uncertain, desperate, or manipulative he is, the more he will have to say to justify himself. It follows that highly argumentative, insistent confessions like Rousseau's and the Underground Man's will be harder to bring to a close than confessions like Augustine's and Moll's.

Michel's confession in *The Immoralist* is interesting on this point because of the unexpected effect it has on one of his confessors. Michel speaks to three old friends, whom he has chosen because they know him well. He apologizes very little for his actions, for he seems to assume his apology is implicit in his choice of an audience. Yet he tells his story so coolly, so unrhetorically, one of the men is disconcerted by his own inability to make objections to Michel and he feels, therefore, that he has been made an accomplice to Michel's "immorality." Had Michel apologized more, analyzed his behavior in more obviously ethical terms, his confessor would have known more readily how to respond.[31] A speaker who feels himself deeply guilty can seek in his confessor a kind of complicity as naturally as he can seek absolution, and it is possible in an ironic confession that an ideal of community could be developed to contain values that are less than idealistic. On the other hand, it would seem that a confession like Michel's which seeks the freedom and renewal of its speaker could also liberate its audience, who would see themselves in a new way because of the confession they have heard. This new knowledge may entail an unexpected sense of guilt, an unadmitted imperfection, the sudden realization of one's own dishonesty or lack of courage; but in the community that is always the hope of a new beginning, this knowledge can be fortifying too, a source of unillusioned strength. However, confessors have their own problems in responding to what they hear and their own interpretations of what they have heard. Although the speaker's rhetoric can be an index of his attitudes and his confessional style, it is no guarantee of his "success" with his audience. Other readers have surely responded to Rouseau with less animus than I have. Confession has its end in community, but confession is open-ended in another sense because community, by its nature, is open too.

Walter J. Ong says that "it is characteristic of our present age that virtually all serious writing tends to be confessional, even drama." Ong does not elaborate on this remark, so it seems he uses *confessional* both in the way Theodor Reik does and in the honorific sense critics use it to describe contemporary writing's

31. See André Gide, *The Immoralist*, trans. Dorothy Bussy (New York: Alfred A. Knopf, 1930), vii–ix.

intimacy, its focus on the self, its resistance to the definitions imposed on the individual by a mass society. However, the title of the article in which Ong makes this remark is more suggestive of confession's real nature—"The Writer's Audience Is Always a Fiction."[32] The writer's identity is a fiction too, in the way that all knowing and telling participate in the conventions of art. Yet, the purpose of a confession is to make these fictions real, and thus confession strains against "mere" art. The speaker does not want his sense of himself to be fictional; he wants to be understood and accepted for what he *is*. The confessional speaker looks, therefore, to an audience that will validate him, toward a community that is not merely an aesthetic relationship but a moral order as well.

32. Walter J. Ong, "The Writer's Audience Is Always a Fiction," *Publications of the Modern Language Association*, XC (January, 1975), 20.

Chapter 3

Three Confessional Novels
Moll Flanders, Notes from Underground, Moby-Dick

I am sure you will pardon this speaking all about myself,—for if I say *so much on that head, be sure all the rest of the world are thinking about themselves ten times as much. Let us speak, though we show our faults and weaknesses,—for it is a sign of strength to be weak, to know it, and out with it,—not in a set way and ostentatiously, though, but incidentally and without premeditation.—But I am falling into my old Foible—preaching.*

HERMAN MELVILLE TO NATHANIEL HAWTHORNE
June 29, 1851

In making his confession, Felix Krull defends himself against simplistic interpretations with a remark that is appropriate to all confessions: "For my own part, I am in agreement with folk wisdom which holds that when two persons do the same thing it is no longer the same."[1] In confessing, Augustine and Rousseau clearly demonstrate this principle; for they try to define their real natures to a carefully defined confessor, but their personal needs and styles are so disparate that each seems to derive a different fulfillment from his confession. Augustine, despite the severity of

1. Thomas Mann, *The Confessions of Felix Krull, Confidence Man,* trans. Denver Lindley (New York: Modern Library, 1965), 112.

his standards and perhaps because of his office in the Church, has more trust in his audience than Rousseau does; within the bounds of charity, Augustine allows his reader a greater freedom and fuller responsibility. Therefore, his is a more successful confession because it fulfills its formal purpose more completely than Rousseau's and fosters a higher quality of human relationship, as it enacts Augustine's need for other people, his recognition of their integrity, his confidence in their love. Rousseau's confession seems to invoke an audience in order to deny its legitimacy, to foster a community that he can spurn in demonstrating his freedom. In formal terms, Rousseau's *Confessions* seem to be a failure.

Yet, in the light of Felix Krull's wisdom, judgments like this have to be made gingerly. Rousseau's needs are not less than Augustine's; his obvious pain and his courage are chastening; his insights and influence have been monumentally important; and sympathy for his self-conception has given his *Confessions* the heroic cast of a defiance we can always honor. The immediate company of heroes may be hard to keep, though; and at some point in hearing a confession, we have to accept or reject the speaker's apology, which is his image of us. In rejecting that apology, however, we need not reject the speaker's definition of himself, nor deny the utility of his confession as it challenges our notions of what constitutes meaning and value in a human life. Augustine wrote his *Confessions* to be useful to others; Rousseau, with more intransigence, did too. And Rousseau may be in fact more useful to the modern reader whose world he more nearly inhabits and defines. I like and admire Augustine more than I do Rousseau, for his humility, rigor, irony, and the more pleasing closure of his *Confessions.* But I would rather reread Rousseau because his *Confessions* are more scandalous, and more challenging because they are less intimidating. Rousseau's *Confessions* are no less useful to me than Augustine's for they can be a form of homeopathy.

So, between the Scylla and Charybdis of community and utility, confessions are judged. And one form of utility—which is a more independent, less formal, more subjective value than community—is explained by Ellrich in his essay on Rousseau. "One of the supreme ironies of romantic literature is precisely the inevitable temptation to 'push back' that the writer's aggression inspires in the reader. With what would seem to be a genius for failure, the romantic writer frequently achieves the contrary of what he has set out to do, and the reader not only fails to take the writer as his model but consciously rejects him as such. Perhaps the writer has, however, achieved a more important aim: he has provoked the reader into an identity duel in which there can be a winner and a loser."[2] In the complexity of our responses to any writer, there seems to be nothing as simple as victory or defeat, but his terms do imply another mode of utility—the usefulness of the confession for the speaker himself. Our own standards of community may be deaf to the rhetoric of the speaker's apology; our own needs may give his confession a meaning he never imagined, a sense that changes his deepest sincerity into irony. When two different persons read *The Confessions of Felix Krull*, it is no longer the same. Yet if one of a speaker's goals in confessing is the catharsis of disburdening himself, he may achieve that end, regardless of the audience's response; and the tone of the final passages of his *Confessions* suggests that Rousseau did achieve some kind of onanistic catharsis in the salon of Mme. d'Egmont.

Judging a confession that informs a novel by the standard of its utility is a more subtle consideration, however. Moll Flanders' confession seems unself-conscious and almost casual, as confessions go. She is clearheaded about herself and straightforward with her audience; and she does want to be useful. The Underground Man is sophisticated, brilliant, and ultimately solipsistic; he is deliberately defiant rather than edifying, and he is so concerned to define an audience he can reject, he ends up talking to no one but himself. For most modern readers, though, *Notes from Underground* is more accessible than *Moll Flanders* and more useful for the questions it raises and the energy it creates. Somewhere between the two stands *Moby-Dick*. Although it contains a wealth of useful information about whales, we read Ishmael's confession

2. Robert J. Ellrich, *Rousseau and His Reader: The Rhetorical Situation of the Major Works*, University of North Carolina Studies in the Romance Languages and Literature, No. 83 (Chapel Hill: University of North Carolina Press, 1969), 77*n*.

in a way we do not read Rousseau's because Rousseau was an historical person and Ishmael is a fictional character. And although they are informed by confessions, *Moll Flanders, Notes from Underground,* and *Moby-Dick* are novels that we can perceive in other ways than we perceive confessions like Augustine's, Rousseau's, or a friend's. *Moll Flanders,* because of its historical and generic provenance, may be quite purely a *confessional novel*; but *Moby-Dick,* in addition to being Ishmael's confession, is also a romance and an anatomy: it is, in fact, as sui generis as *Ulysses.*

Nonetheless, as a standard for understanding and judging these novels, community still applies, because it defines the purpose of each speaker's direct address and relationship to the reader. What these three novels demonstrate is that no one makes a confession primarily to be useful, but simply to be; and what they share, for all their variety, is confession's formal purpose of creating a community in which the speaker can have his being. Reading them as confessions, moreover, allows us to entertain some answers to problems each of these novels has posed. *Moll Flanders* is a less ironic novel than many readers have thought if we understand it in terms of the audience Moll consciously addresses; and she herself becomes a more interesting character for some of her political views. *Notes from Underground,* on the other hand, is less nihilistic if we understand it in terms of the kind of community the narrator's polemic truly fosters, before he himself refuses to enter that community. And Ishmael's conception of freedom is less "shoreless" and more companionable if we remember that its initial premise is his request that we call him Ishmael. Recognizing him as the outsider, we give him a place in a community that resembles the one he had begun to form with Queequeg.

The central, definitive preoccupation of the novel has been the nature of individual human experience in time, and at the heart of the confession is also this concern for the speaker's temporal life. In this sense, confession may be one of the purest forms of the novel, or one of those primary human impulses that novelists have incorporated to make the novel what Lawrence calls "the one bright book of life." Yet one of the novel's great strengths is that it is not a pure form. And beyond its definitive intention to define the self in terms of a community, confession accommodates various impurities itself. They therefore complement each other in our discussions of them and of ourselves as their readers.

Moll Flanders is an outsider from the moment of her illegitimate birth in Newgate prison until her return from penal exile in America, when she is in her sixties. She confesses as both a rehabilitated criminal and a religious penitent, since, in Newgate again, she has undergone a conversion. The novel that bears Moll's name is therefore a natural starting point, but Moll is a hard case. It is often very difficult for the modern reader to hear her confession as sincere because Moll herself seems so smug. As Ian Watt says: "We cannot today believe that so intelligent a man as Defoe should have viewed either his heroine's economic attitudes or her pious protestations with anything other than derision."[3] There are more contradictions to Moll than her economy and piety, however. She is a picaro who writes a spiritual autobiography, a famous thief who has had a score of children, a woman who has passed as a man, and she makes her confession under the pseudonym for which she has been most famous in the underworld. Naturally, Moll evokes extreme responses. Dorothy Van Ghent, who sees her as a completely ironic character, says Moll has the "immense and seminal reality of an Earth Mother" but speaks in the "platitudes and stereotypes and absurdities of a morality suitable to a wasteland world."[4] Arnold Kettle is more tolerant of Moll, whom he sees as a victim of economic circumstances, and more comfortable with the question of the novel's irony, which he does not try to answer. "The question 'How far is Defoe's irony intentional?' is not really a fruitful question."[5] In the middle is another formula-

3. Ian Watt, *The Rise of the Novel* (Berkeley: University of California Press, 1964), 127.

4. Dorothy Van Ghent, *The English Novel: Form and Function* (New York: Harper and Row, 1953), 43.

5. Arnold Kettle, "In Defence of Moll Flanders," in Daniel Defoe, *Moll Flanders*, ed. Edward Kelly (New York: W. W. Norton, 1972), 395. Two other excellent studies of Moll's identity are Terence Martin, "The Unity

tion of Watt's which suggests again that the problem with Moll may lie in us and in the way we read her. "*Moll Flanders* is undoubtedly an ironic object, but it is not a work of irony."[6]

Ralph W. Rader extends Watt's insight by saying that *Moll Flanders'* ironies arise from our failure to understand its real form. "Let us say what has often been said but never fully understood: *Moll Flanders* is an imitation of a real autobiography." Rader says further: "Defoe's aim was to simulate both the intelligibility and effect of a true story. . . . A kind of story that I would call a naïve incoherent autobiography, a story really told by a real person like Moll. There are no well-known examples of the genre, because such works are by definition deficient in art."[7] By art, Rader must mean polish, for *Moll Flanders* is not wholly incoherent or deficient in form if it is understood to be Moll's confession and therefore informed by her intention to identify herself to the community she needs and wants to serve. Understanding Moll's confessional purpose does not smooth out the texture of her narrative nor fill in her story's lacunae; it does, however, allow us to see that she is not so naïve as she may seem. Moreover, her sense of herself and her specific need for the community she addresses are unusual enough to make her confession quite different from those of Augustine and Rousseau and are thereby illuminating of the possible shapes the confessional impulse can take.

The crisis from which Moll's confession issues is not so much a crisis of identity as a religious conversion; and unlike Augustine and Rousseau, she does not write from the midst of that crisis in order to resolve it. The events of her life have resolved the crisis for her. After her conversion in Newgate, Moll and her Lancashire

---

of *Moll Flanders,*" *Modern Language Quarterly,* XXII (1961), 115–24. Reprinted in Defoe, *Moll Flanders.* And William J. Krier, "A Courtesy Which Grants Integrity: A Literary Reading of *Moll Flanders,*" *Journal of English Literary History,* XXXVIII (September, 1971), 397–410.

6. Watt, *Rise of the Novel,* 130.

7. Ralph W. Rader, "Defoe, Richardson, Joyce and the Concept of Form in the Novel," in William Matthews and Ralph W. Rader (eds.), *Autobiography, Biography, and the Novel* (Los Angeles: William Andrews Clark Memorial Library, University of California, 1973), 39, 41.

husband go into exile in America, prosper there, and return to England where Moll now lives as a "gentlewoman." Her prosperity itself has validated her survival and religious turn; she is already living within the community she addresses; and she assumes that her audience will see the connection between her conversion and success. Consequently, Moll writes with a greater distance on herself than we usually expect from a confessional speaker. She also writes without the profound sense of the ontological aspect of her nature that is in Augustine and Rousseau. This lack of ontological awareness makes Moll's confession seem unself-conscious, but it is not. Moll does not ask her audience to recognize her identity; she asks it to recognize her right to it, the freedom she needs to maintain it, and her attempt to justify herself by being useful. Her desire to be useful makes Moll's confession more apologetic than confessional, and it is in what she apologizes for that Moll most clearly tells us who she is.

It may be hard to hear Moll's apology because we expect her to feel more sorrow or guilt for her past sins. Yet given her success and her age, intense compunction for every misdeed of her long life would seem unlikely or unnatural; in Moll particularly, it could also seem hypocritical. One of her most attractive virtues, and one of the reasons she has survived, is Moll's strong resistance to the temptations of guilt. In describing her stay in the Mint, Moll says:

> It was indeed a Subject of strange Reflections to me to see Men who were overwhelm'd in perplex'd Circumstances, who were reduced some Degrees below being Ruin'd; whose families were Objects of their own Terror and other Peoples Charity; yet while a Penny lasted, nay, even beyond it, endeavoring to drown their Sorrow in their Wickedness; Heaping up more guilt upon themselves, labouring to forget former things, which now it was the proper time to remember, making more Work for Repentance, and Sinning on, as a Remedy for Sin past.
>
> But it is none of my Talent to preach; these men were

> too wicked, even for me; there was something horrid and absurd in their way of Sinning, for it was all a force even upon themselves; they did not only act against Conscience, but against Nature; they put a Rape upon their Temper to drown the Reflections, which their circumstances continually gave them.[8]

Though such characters and behavior appeal to Dostoevsky in a later age, they do not reflect Moll, who is neither a compulsive nor a self-destructive personality. Moreover, her sins are not absurd, and the ones she does apologize for most emphatically are those she commits against her own nature.

Moll says she hesitates to preach not only because "it is none of my Talent" but also because she believes that her audience understands her quite well already, that it resembles her and agrees with her, and that she can make her points quickly. Less confident of himself, the Underground Man will preach to his audience quite strenuously; and so, in his own way, will Ishmael. Moll, of course, preaches too, since preaching is a natural mode of apology. Nonetheless, her attitude toward her preaching is important because it indicates her trust in her audience. With a similar trust in their audiences, Gatsby will not preach or even apologize to Nick Carraway, and Thomas Sutpen will not apologize to General Compson; like Moll, they assume their apology is implicit in their choice of a confessor. Even if their assumption is wrong, it is the basis of their confessional style. This refusal to apologize also characterizes Gatsby as shallow and unreflective, and Sutpen as narrow and obsessive, but not every speaker whose apology is muted can be so characterized. Leo Tolstoy's *A Confession* is short, relatively simple, and almost as unapologetic as a religious confession can be. He wrote it after instead of during the crisis of faith he describes, and he addresses it to an audience he knows very well—his class, "our circle," "people on our level of education." By the time he writes, Tolstoy has renounced the life of "our circle," but he has not renounced his identity as an aristocrat, so he addresses his

8. Defoe, *Moll Flanders*, 52.

natural community in order to instruct it. Like Moll, Tolstoy wants to be useful.

Neither Moll nor Tolstoy is so naïve as to exclude the possibility of an inimical reader, one who will not accept them in terms of their intentions. The "strange children" Tolstoy defines as his antagonists are the community of writers he once belonged to, the artists who justified themselves as teachers without knowing what they had to teach.[9] Moll defines her antagonists as the skeptics who do not accept her conversion and would prefer her story to be a "compleat Tragedy." Here she recounts the experience in Newgate that so dramatically changes her life.

> This may be thought inconsistent in it self, and wide from the Business of this Book; Particularly, I reflect that many of those who may be pleas'd and diverted with the Relation of the wild and wicked part of my Story, may not relish this, which is really the best part of my Life, the most Advantageous to myself, and the most instructive to others; such however will I hope allow me the liberty to make my Story compleat: It would be a severe Satyr on such, to say that they do not relish the Repentance as much as they do the Crime; and that they had rather the History were a compleat Tragedy, as it was very likely to have been.[10]

Moll does not ask for much ratification. What she does ask for is "liberty," and she attributes to her audience a generosity that she always displays in return. Moll never "satirizes" her adversaries, as do Rousseau and the Underground Man.

Defoe, aware of his novel's potential readership, tries to prepare that audience for Moll's confessional style through a fictional editor who makes Moll's confession appear to be real. Defoe admits

9. Leo Tolstoy, *A Confession*, in John Bayley (ed.), *The Portable Tolstoy*, (Harmondsworth, England: Penguin Books, 1978), 667, 671. For a different opinion of Tolstoy's rhetoric, see Henri Troyat, *Tolstoy*, trans. Nancy Amphoux (Garden City, N.Y.: Doubleday, 1967), 396.

10. Defoe, *Moll Flanders*, 228.

that Moll will be hard to hear properly, so he has the editor's preface absorb some the apology we would expect to hear from Moll herself if she were more anxious about her reader. Although the editor has not been Moll's confessor, he has read her well and he understands her intention. Therefore, he tries to diminish the scandal in her narrative, to neutralize some of the anticipated skepticism, and to define the community in which Moll has taken her place. He says, for instance, that he has cleaned up some of the Newgate language and deleted "some of the vicious parts of her Life, which cou'd not be modestly told." He acts because he realizes Moll wants to be more edifying than entertaining and because he knows that such an intention seems unusual from a narrator "Born in Newgate, and during a Life of Continu'd Variety for Threescore Years, besides her Childhood, was Twelve Year a *Whore,* five times a *Wife* (whereof once to her own Brother) Twelve Year a *Thief,* Eight Year a Transported *Felon* in *Virginia,* at last grew *Rich,* liv'd *Honest,* and died a *Penitent,*" as the subtitle says. He defines the proper audience of Moll's confession as those readers who are more interested in Moll's end than in her career. "But as this Work is chiefly recommended to those who know how to Read it, and how to make the good uses of it, which the story all along recommends to them, so it is to be hop'd that such Readers will be more pleased with the Moral than the Fable, with the Application than with the Relation, and with the End of the Writer than with the Life of the Person Written of." This editor also admits to Moll's limitations. He says that she has grown "very Rich" and "very old" and that she has become "not so extraordinary a Penitent as she was at first; it seems only that she spoke with abhorence of her former Life, and of every Part of it."[11] This information aside, the editor does not say anything about Moll that she does not say herself. He asks us, as she does, to define ourselves morally, to hear her out in terms of her intention, and to accept in her the freedom she accepts in us.

If Moll speaks "with abhorence of her former Life," she has

11. *Ibid.*, 3, 4, 6.

good reason to: her former life has been horrible. It has not made her cynical, however, and the trust she displays in her audience also indicates her dependence on their community. If she is to be as useful as she wants to be, she must be accepted as such; to win this acceptance, she continually defers to their judgment and experience, even when she is discussing the parts of her life about which she can be most authoritative—crime in the streets and her conversion.

> On the other hand, every Branch of my Story, if duly consider'd, may be useful to honest People, and afford a due Caution to People like some sort or other to Guard against the like Surprizes, and to have their eyes about them when they have to do with Strangers of any kind, for 'tis very seldom that some Snare or other is not in their way. The Moral indeed of all History is left to be gather'd by the Senses and Judgment of the Reader; I am not Qualified to preach to them, let the Experience of one Creature compleatly Wicked, and compleatly Miserable be a Storehouse of useful warning to those that read.
>
> . . . .
>
> I am not capable of reading Lectures of Instruction to any Body, but I relate this in the very manner in which things then appear'd to me, as far as I am able; but infinitely short of the lively impressions which they made on my Soul at that time; indeed those Impressions are not to be explained by words, or if they are, I am not Mistress of Words enough to express them; It must be the Work of every sober Reader to make just Reflections on them, as their own Circumstances may direct; and without Question, this is what every one at sometime or other may feel something of: I mean a clearer Sight into things to come, than they had here, and a dark view of their own Concern in them.[12]

12. *Ibid.*, 210, 225.

This is Moll's version of the community of charity that Augustine depends on to hear his confession, and her dependence on such a community is the natural result of the circumstances of her conversion, which happens while she awaits hanging in Newgate. She admits that she would not have been converted if she had not been caught, and she experiences the sequence of stupor and regeneration that characterizes conversions of her kind. She says also that "for the first time I felt any real signs of Repentance" and the "incomprehensible Additions" of the word "Eternity."[13] Yet she stresses that three people were as instrumental to her change of heart as her impending death was: her Lancashire husband, in Newgate himself, for whom Moll still feels affection and a guilty responsibility; her old "Governess," whose love for Moll and whose grief over Moll's sentence have led her to make her own conversion; and the generous, compassionate cleric who has counseled Moll to repent. Conversions themselves are acts of community; when Moll confesses, she still has need for a religious community's support.

As the passages quoted above indicate, Moll is not completely unself-conscious. In fact, there is a certain cunning to her rhetorical ploy of admitting to the insufficiency of her style in the same breath that she honors the audience's competence of judgment. There may also be some cunning in the way she considers her own life representative of her times, for this too encourages her reader to accept her on her own terms. Most individuals who make a religious confession think of themselves as representative or typical, for their conversions do typify them.[14] Yet Moll also has a broader sense of herself, and she understands that the confessional impulse has a reach beyond the merely religious community. The life she has lived in "Continu'd Variety" has taught her the importance of intimacy, a need that lies behind any confession of whatever kind; and in explaining that need Moll invokes a much wider audience than those who have shared only her religious experience: "For let

13. *Ibid.*, 225.

14. See G. A. Starr, *Defoe and Spiritual Autobiography* (Princeton, N.J.: Princeton University Press, 1965), 14.

them say what they please of our Sex not being able to keep a Secret, my life is a plain conviction to me of the contrary; but be it our Sex, or the Man's Sex, a Secret of Moment should always have a Confident, a bosom Friend, to whom we may Communicate the Joy of it, or the Grief of it, be it which it will, or it will be a double weight upon the Spirits, and perhaps become even insupportable in itself; and this I appeal to all human Testimony for the Truth of."[15]

Seldom in her life has Moll had the confidants with whom she can be simply herself. Except in her relations with some understanding older women—mother figures and her actual mother—Moll has had to withhold herself, lie, or connive to survive in a world determined by men. Most of her marriages have been the arrangements of convenience or necessity rather than love. So, as a mother figure herself, Moll wants to take advantage of the intimacy she has created in her confession to advise women that, in lieu of the possibility of intimacy, they can play the game men have played against them.

> Thus I convinc'd her, that the Men had their Advantage of our Sex in the Affair of Marriage, upon the supposition of there being such Choice to be had, and of the Women being so easie, it is only owing to this, that the Women wanted Courage to maintain their Ground, and to Play their Part.
>
> . . . .
>
> I cannot but remind the Ladies here how much they place themselves below the common Station of a Wife, which if I may be allow'd not to be Partial is low enough already; I *say* they place themselves below their common Station, and prepare their own Mortifications, by their submitting so to be insulted by the Men beforehand, which I confess I see no Necessity of.
>
> . . . .

15. Defoe, *Moll Flanders*, 254.

> She is always Married too soon who gets a bad Husband, and she is never Married too late who gets a good one: In a word, there is no Woman, *Deformity, or lost Reputation excepted,* but if she manages well, may be Marry'd safely one time or another; but if she precipitates herself, it is ten Thousand to one but she is undone.[16]

Moll herself is an example of precipitousness, of subsequent good management, and even of the possibility that a "lost Reputation" can be overcome. Her words grow strong here, without any apologies for their inadequacy, because she is arguing for two of her deepest beliefs: personal freedom and the benefits of marriage. In her own mind, Moll has been most free when she has been well married, as she is at the moment. She does not celebrate his individuality for its own sake; her confession argues for the kind of freedom community provides her. And Moll's most powerful metaphor of this kind of community is marriage. Marriage is also a powerful metaphor of community in *Moby-Dick* and *Absalom, Absalom!*

The sins Moll apologizes for most explicitly are the sins she has committed against marriage and the errors that being on her own has led her to make. Like Rousseau, she gives away all her children; yet this is an act in which she takes no pride, she never tries to explain it away, and at one point she refers to it as "Murther" as she warns other women against doing it.[17] She is also deeply remorseful about her marriage to Robin because her love for his older brother causes her to think of herself as both adulterous and incestuous. Moll learns to accommodate adultery because it is a sin against society rather than nature, but her innocent marriage to her half-brother repulses her. Incest is as unnatural as excessive guilt, and both are far more serious than promiscuity.[18] The fact that she takes her career as a thief more seriously than her life as

16. *Ibid.*, 58, 59, 60.
17. *Ibid.*, 135.
18. See David Goldknopf, *The Life of the Novel* (Chicago: University of Chicago Press, 1972), 57.

a whore is also significant, and she is quite apologetic for her most recent crimes. Moll works hard at justifying the necessity that drives her to steal, and explaining her early confusion and distaste, her self-serving compassion for her victims, and then her growing avarice. Nonetheless, the reason that she remained a thief for so long is clear: the underworld community gave her what the middle-class world could not—the security she had always sought in marriage and the approval she now seeks in confession.

In judging Moll, the most crucial question we can ask is, why does she confess? The only answers that seem reasonable are the ones she gives herself: to maintain her freedom and to be useful. Because of her pseudonym, and perhaps the controversial nature of her confession, she can gain no immediate material advantage; yet by using her pseudonym, she can use the publicity it has earned to give her story and her instruction greater authority. If Moll says nothing ontologically profound about herself, it is because there is nothing profound to say. She is a simple character and shallow in the way that picaresque characters naturally are.[19] By virtue of this simplicity, she has survived in a world that is marked by constant and uncontrollable change, that is quite uncertain about class distinctions and social identities, that rewards mobility and honors appearance. Moll's adaptability is remarkable; she survives at least two intense crises before her conversion—her marriage to Robin and to her half-brother—and she develops a great facility for disguises and playing roles. Yet Moll's innate sense of her own identity is so firm, she never loses herself in these circumstances or games. She believes her problems arise not so much from within herself as from the conditions of the world she inhabits. If she criticizes the rites of courtship and the poverty that compels her to steal with more fervor than she shows in criticizing her own weaknesses, she does this with the trust that her audience will realize she has made her choices in order to survive and that her confession is an attempt to make her survival useful to others.

19. See Robert B. Heilman, "Variations of Picaresque (*Felix Krull*)," *Sewanee Review*, LXVI (Autumn, 1958), 547–77.

Ian Watt somewhat underestimates Moll even as he tries to praise her. "Her wisdom is not impressive; it is at best a low atavistic kind wholly directed to the problems of survival; but nothing could be more impressive than her energy, and it too has a moral premise, a kind of inarticulate and yet fortifying stoicism."[20] Wisdom is a very high standard by which to judge a first-person narrator; it may not even be a quality that we look for in the characters we love because wisdom suggests their finality, which gives them the distance of Augustine's God. And of a confessional speaker especially, wisdom is an inappropriate measure. Furthermore, Watt's assessment of Moll implies a preference for the grander, tragic characters of the nineteenth-century novel, like Emma Bovary and Anna Karenina. However, in many ways, the eighteenth-century novel bears more resemblance to novels of the twentieth century than to those of the nineteenth, and Moll is more fairly seen in the company of Molly Bloom and Lena Grove. Indeed, her most fitting counterparts may be in Bertolt Brecht's plays—the women of *Mother Courage* and *The Good Woman of Setzuan*, and Grusha of *The Caucasian Chalk Circle*. These characters are not only survivors, they are also "naturals" who have become increasingly important in the modern literature that is skeptical of too much self-consciousness.[21] Finally, Moll's morality includes more than stoicism. It also includes her intention to teach us how difficult it can be to achieve the freedom she wants and how much easier it is to be good when one is secure.

Moll's intention is simple and direct; her trust in her audience is carefully defined and generous; and her sense of herself and her life's meaning allows her to end her confession looking toward the future. She and her husband "resolve to spend the Remainder of our Years in sincere Penitence, for the wicked Lives we have lived."[22] As Moll's confession, *Moll Flanders* is not a "work of irony." If we have made the novel an "ironic object," we may have

20. Watt, *Rise of the Novel*, 132.

21. See Richard Ellmann, *James Joyce* (London: Oxford University Press, 1959), 329–30.

22. Defoe, *Moll Flanders*, 268.

done so because we have come to trust the kind of irony we see in the Underground Man as an absolute standard of truth and authenticity. Perhaps the greatest irony in this trust is on us: we accept the Underground Man more readily because he is a casualty rather than a survivor.

Although there is no particular "age of confessions," individual confessions themselves can illuminate the conditions of important historical moments, especially moments of significant transition. *Moll Flanders* reflects the rise of secularism, capitalism, and individualism that marked the early eighteenth century; it also reflects the rise of the novel itself from the popular conventions of the rogue's biography and from the traditions of the Protestant confession.[23] *Notes from Underground* issues from the postromantic confusion that also fostered the development of the dramatic monologue, a form with which modern confessional novels have much in common.[24] And Dostoevsky's novel seems particularly important as the progenitor of many subsequent confessional narratives that explore existential isolation, modern anxiety, and the dissolution of human community. The Underground Man is a brilliant prophet of "the fate of pleasure" and the natural history of modern loneliness.[25] He has no real intentional audience, no hope or faith in the community his confession can create. He is always talking to himself. The "gentlemen" he addresses are a fiction he has devised only to repudiate, and he is unaware of the "editor" who has presented his "notes" to a real audience. Like Rousseau, the Underground Man insists that who he is, is what he says; he is not to be taken for what he does, but at his word alone. Yet what he finally means to the reader is the complicated result of the relationships that Dostoevsky has created between the narrator, his gentlemen, the editor, and the reader. And to the reader

23. See Watt, *Rise of the Novel*, Chap. 1, especially.

24. See Robert Langbaum, *The Poetry of Experience*, (New York: W. W. Norton, 1963), 9–37.

25. See Lionel Trilling, *Beyond Culture* (New York: Viking Press, 1968), 57–87.

these relationships come as something of a surprise (which the editor's initial, ambivalent footnote does not fully prepare us for), when the Underground Man comes to the end of his polemic and begins to draw away from the audience he has addressed so intensely throughout Part One. In Chapter Eleven, the narrator suddenly discounts his belief in everything he has said. He mimics a perfect critique of his whole performance and goes on to say, "Confessions of the kind that I intend to begin setting forth are not published and are not given to other people to read," which means that they are not confessions at all, but a diary or mirror exercise. He says further:

> I, on the other hand, am writing only for myself, and I state once and for all that if I appear to be writing as though I were addressing readers, it is just simply for show, because it's easier for me to write that way. It is a form, just an irrelevant form, for I am never going to have readers. I have already stated that.
>
> I don't want to feel restricted by anything in editing my notes. I am not going to introduce any system or order. I'll write down whatever I recall.
>
> How about this, for instance: couldn't you split hairs and ask me: "If you really don't expect readers, why are you making pacts with yourself, and on paper yet, namely, that you are not going to introduce any system or order, that you will write whatever you recall, and so on, and so on? Why are you explaining? Why are you making excuses?"
>
> "Well, you figure it out," I answer.[26]

It is not hard to figure out from this apology and the following notes of reminiscence that the Underground Man's need for an audience's recognition is constant, essential, and desperate, if he is to realize himself. Yet he cannot admit to needing a community of any kind because he does not want "to feel restricted by any-

26. Fyodor Dostoevsky, *Notes from Underground*, ed. Robert G. Durgy, trans. Serge Shishkoff (New York: Thomas Y. Crowell, 1969), 37–38.

thing . . . any system or order"; so he cannot entrust his identity to anything but a fictionalized audience that he conceives to exploit and repudiate as an "irrevelant form."

Dostoevsky's intentions for *Notes from Underground* reveal themselves as different from his narrator's and quite complex, and these intentions are worked out not only in the differences between the gentlemen and the real reader but also in the temporal relationship between Parts One and Two. By placing the polemic first, Dostoevsky sets the reader up to be manipulated into two very different reactions to the Underground Man. If the polemic of Part One were to come in its proper chronological place, after the notes of reminiscence in Part Two, the polemic would lose much of its cogency and meaning. But faced with it immediately, the reader cannot be sure of the narrator's real motive in confessing, of Dostoevsky's distance from his character, or of his own status in the confessional audience. This uncertainty allows Dostoevsky to make his own argument through the narrator before the narrator is allowed to reveal himself more fully and raise questions in the reader's mind about his authority. For if the Underground Man is eventually undermined by his own failures, he is initially a convincing spokesman against the rationalism Dostoevsky finds so dangerous.

As the natural vehicle of the outsider, the confession is a perfect mode in which to attack the rationalist social planners, the gentlemen, whose systems and progressive ideals not only faslify human nature but oversimplify the meaning of human community by placing order above freedom. Like Rousseau, the Underground Man defies that order because it does not requite his needs. But unlike Rousseau, the Underground Man cannot imagine being accepted for what he has to say. This imaginative failure to recognize the need for human intimacy is what undoes the Underground Man, despite the brilliance of his rhetoric.

The crisis that motivates the Underground Man's confession is, like Rousseau's, a crisis of isolation. Confessions that are built on a religious model, like Augustine's and Moll's, are grounded on a conversion. Secular confessions, like Rousseau's and the Underground Man's, are often grounded on a kind of "deconversion," a turning away from the world and into the self. But in the polemic, the Underground Man never treats his isolation as a crisis; he treats it as a form of liberation and as an advantage for the superior insight it affords. Like Rousseau, he writes against a conventional audience, explicitly trying to dominate the gentlemen as though to win a debate, implicitly trying to define himself by his opposition. The outsider may not know exactly who he is, but he has a clear sense of what he is not. If he cannot be as sure as Moll Flanders of who will constitute his sympathetic audience, he has learned in self-defense the features of his enemies. But because he is making a confession, the Underground Man seems to be talking past the gentlemen on purpose, to another audience he cannot yet identify, for it is an audience he will create in the process of defining himself. The reader's uncertain position at this point lends to the narrative the excitement of collusion; for the reader knows from the start that he is not one of the gentlemen addressed so rudely. He knows himself that he is harder to define, and he wants the freedom of his own response.

To dominate the gentlemen and define himself, the Underground Man makes no apology about his honesty or humility, and he never overtly courts his audience or seeks its sympathy. On the contrary, he argues his case with great self-confidence in order to destroy the rationalist position; and he begins his attack in the first sentence—"I am a sick man . . . I am a nasty man"—putting off the sympathetic response his illness could evoke by immediately changing his plea to a much less sympathetic cause. Then he admits to a lie he could never have been suspected of, and in doing so, he indicates how enthusiastically he will manipulate the conventional expectations of his discourse. He makes himself a difficult man to answer because he pursues his argument with such speed, through so many shifts of tone and attitude, that there is no logical way to respond. For instance, after arguing quite seriously about the problems of acting on the basis of a primary cause, he immediately begins his ironic celebration of the "loafer": "Why, that's a title and a purpose, that's a whole career. Don't joke, it's so."[27] And these remarks slide through a parody of the aesthete's devotion to "the sublime and the beautiful" into the serious argument that freedom itself, whatever its result, is more advantageous than the pursuit of enlightened self-interest.

Although he cannot be readily anticipated at any turn in his performance, the narrator nonetheless keeps silencing the gentlemen by anticipating their objections and transforming them into the evidence of his own authority.

> "Perhaps it also will not be understood," you'll chime in, with a smirk, "by those who have never been slapped in the face"—and in this way politely hint that at some time in my life I also may have received a slap in the face and that's the reason I speak like an expert. I'll bet that is what you are thinking. But don't worry, gentlemen, I have never been slapped, though I don't care at all what you may think about that. And perhaps I even regret that during my lifetime I did not give out enough slaps myself. But enough, not another word on this subject that interests you so.[28]

Not even Rousseau is this manipulative, and the Underground Man neutralizes insults and *ad hominem* objections by defiantly admitting to every fault he knows himself to have. For instance: "You laugh? Delighted, gentlemen. My jokes are, of course, tasteless, uneven, confused, self-mistrusting. But that is because I don't respect myself. After all, can a conscious man respect himself at all?" The reader at this point is inclined to answer, yes, a conscious man can respect himself, because the narrator seems to know himself so well and to have such clear command of his own argument and energy. He can make even pointless jokes: "I am going to live to be sixty myself. I'll live to be seventy! I'll live to be eighty! . . . Wait! Let me catch my breath."[29]

These rhetorical stunts have a very serious purpose, however.

27. *Ibid.*, 18.
28. *Ibid.*, 12.
29. *Ibid.*, 15, 5.

For in delivering an apology in which he refuses to apologize, the Underground Man must make himself the most convincing demonstration of the case he is trying to make against mere rationality. He has to "authorize" himself in a way that neither Moll nor Augustine has to, because he is defying the community he addresses directly.[30] In opposing rational systems, he cannot propose an alternative system, he can only propose himself. Moreover, because he does not want to win from his audience the kind of approbation Rousseau needs from his, the Underground Man seems healthier than Rousseau, less self-centered, more interested in the truth of his argument than in the success of his self-justification. What he seems to offer, beyond the performance itself, is a concept of human nature that is truer to his own experience and probably appealing to anyone else who has found himself excluded in any way by rationalistic orders.

> Take me, for instance; quite naturally I want to live so as to satisfy my entire capacity to live and not only satisfy my reasoning capacity, which is perhaps a piddling twentieth part of my total capacity to live. What does reason know? Reason knows only what it has managed to learn (I guess there are some things that it will never learn; perhaps that's no consolation, but why shouldn't we mention it?), while human nature acts as a whole, with everything it's got, consciously and unconsciously, and though it blunders, it lives. I suspect, gentlemen, that you are looking at me with pity . . . it [desire] may be more advantageous than all the advantages even in a case where it causes us evident injury and contradicts the most sensible conclusions of our reason about advantages, because in any event it preserves what is most important and most precious to us, that is, our personality and individuality.[31]

30. See Jean Starobinski, "The Style of Autobiography," in Seymour Chatman (ed.), *Literary Style: A Symposium* (London: Oxford University Press, 1971), 291.

31. Dostoevsky, *Notes from Underground*, 27–28.

The Underground Man's statement expresses his holistic idea of human nature. He insists that human identity itself, "our personality and individuality," is an ultimate value far more important than rational explanations of it. He implicitly encourages an exploratory personal freedom by honoring experience over ideas. And his intensity here has a bracing, prophetic ring.

The very presence of the gentlemen, who are the Underground Man's counterparts of Augustine's "strange children," indicates that it is Dostoevsky's design to give his narrator, at least at this point, a legitimate prophetic authority. These gentlemen are so easily mastered that the reader is encouraged to distance himself from them and move closer to the narrator and to the state of consciousness in which he has discovered himself and his difficult freedom. Since the Underground Man hopes to expose the fallacy of rationalist assumptions and counter their abstractions with the evidence of his own life, it is a perfect strategy that he deny the rationalists' very existence. For this denial thwarts a rational expectation and becomes a paradox that, like all the other paradoxes he explores, keeps his argument open-ended and his identity free of easy resolutions. This denial also gives the reader a sense of privileged participation at this point and heightens his own self-consciousness. As Robert M. Adams says of the effect of open-ended forms:

> A characteristic, then, of one sort of open-formed work is the direct and unmediated quality of its relation to the audience. By imputing to its reader no character at all, or condition purely negative, the work in closed form disguises or minimizes its essentially relativist relation to the reader. Works in the open form make this relativism explicit. They often imply an image of man as an essentially divided and self-antagonistic creature. Although he may be ignorant of this fact at first, the work brings him to a realization of it; and to do so it must stand at once closer to the reader and further from its own actions or characters. Its proper effect always precludes simple identification between reader and

> character; an element of self-consciousness enters into the proper reaction to the work in open form.[32]

Adams' description of the effect of an open form is a fairly accurate, if moderate, description of what the Underground Man seems to stand for and would wish his audience, if he had one, to recognize about both him and themselves: not the "simple identification" Rousseau requires, but the self-consciousness that admits to "the image of man as an essentially divided and self-antagonistic creature." This is an image of man that Augustine could understand, and it respects the reader's individuality with something like the generosity Moll Flanders displays. Moreover, the open literary form, projected to moral and political ends, is implicitly a model of the kind of community in which the Underground Man could have a public life—a community of self-conscious, "relative," mutually independent individuals, seeking their realization in experience. This community has certain paradoxical properties, of course, but it is not a wholly impossible ideal.

Before the unfolding of Part Two, the narrator sounds like what he wants to be: a superior intelligence in radical opposition to modern society. Moreover, he has convinced the reader, given to him by Dostoevsky, of the validity of his argument against the rationalist gentlemen. This effort is not the end of *Notes from Underground*, however, for Dostoevsky has more to reveal about his narrator and a serious qualification to apply. The reader comes to understand this qualification as he is allowed to acquire some distance on the narrator by seeing him in circumstances where other audiences have met him and been allowed to respond to his performance. These encounters reveal that the Underground Man's motive for confessing is not so disinterested as it has seemed; they also prove that the strategy he adopts for the polemic is not simply a brilliant rhetorical technique but the result of a compulsion that has determined his whole life. This man with no name—who says he "slavishly adored the conventional in everything con-

32. Robert M. Adams, *Strains of Discord: Studies in Literary Openness* (Ithaca, N.Y.: Cornell University Press, 1958), 291.

cerning outward appearance" and whose fantasy life is often an act of plagiarism—cannot entrust himself to anyone else.[33] Instead he plays roles and he hopes, by the strength of his performance, to cast everyone he meets into the role of an audience that will validate his new persona, which is not his real identity. Moll Flanders has played roles; but she has never mistaken her roles for herself, and her life has been by many standards a success. But the Underground Man has been driven underground because his roles have all failed. He could neither sustain his own part nor compel his audiences to maintain theirs. In retrospect, therefore, the polemic is to be seen as a superior version of the kind of performance he has been giving with much less success throughout his life. And the polemic is a success because he has invented an audience that cannot respond to deny him.[34]

One of Dostoevsky's fundamental points is that the narrator, who argues so well for the freedom of the individual at almost any cost, cannot be free alone. He must be free before someone who will confirm his freedom as the basis of his identity, and he has to rely on a form like the confession. Yet because he violates confession's formal intention by confessing to no one at all, he ends up without the freedom to stop writing. What undermines even his legitimate insights are the revelations about himself that he does not know he is making. Because form and system are irrelevant to him, he cannot recognize the patterns in his own life, which the reader sees so well.

The first major episode of Part Two is the narrator's least successful attempt to create an audience—out of the officer in the tavern who refuses to recognize his presence and moves him like a piece of furniture. The narrator has no immediate response because he fears the "literary" strategies he first considers will be jeered and the *point d'honneur* misunderstood. Some years later he writes a satire against the officer, which goes unpublished be-

33. Dostoevsky, *Notes from Underground*, 42.

34. A different argument for the integrity of Parts 1 and 2 is made by Ralph E. Matlaw, "Structure and Integration in *Notes from Underground*," *Publications of the Modern Language Association*, LXXII (1958), 101–80.

cause the particular convention is not then in vogue. Later still, he writes a "charming" letter, demanding an apology and proposing a duel, which he hopes will reveal the fineness of his sensibility and move the officer to "come running to me with outstretched arms and offer me his friendship. And how great that would be! We would have such a life, such a life! He would protect me by his stature; I would ennoble him with my progressiveness, and, well . . . ideas."[35] He never sends the letter, of course; he finally decides he must settle for another form of recognition, without any hope of a "life" together, by bumping into the man on the Nevsky. Yet even this physical response, years too late, involves a role and reliance on convention, because the Underground Man has to dress up to play the part of a boulevardier.

> The previous night I had definitely resolved not to carry out my pernicious intention and to leave everything alone, and with this in mind I went to the Nevsky one last time to see how I was going to leave all this alone. Suddenly, three paces away from my enemy, I unexpectedly made my decision, closed my eyes and—we knocked together solidly, shoulder to shoulder! I did not yield an inch and passed by on an absolutely equal footing. He did not even turn around, and pretended that he had not noticed; but it was only a pretense, I am sure of it. To this very day I am sure of it. Naturally, I got the worst of it; he was stronger, but that was not what mattered. What mattered was that I had attained my goal, upheld my dignity; I had not retreated a single step and had publicly placed myself on an equal social footing with him.[36]

The narrator's claim that the officer has pretended not to notice is itself a pretense that is now the narrator's only means of "controlling" the officer's response. What the reader notices himself is the narrator's self-deception and a kind of apology that he has never made before. The flip self-deprecation of the polemic has become

35. Dostoevsky, *Notes from Underground*, 49.
36. *Ibid.*, 53.

a more strident insistence that discloses the narrator's need for both personal acceptance and a sustaining belief in his own intelligence, even when he is talking to himself.

The Underground Man is a bit more successful in subsequent episodes as he creates situations that allow him to talk to someone else. He goes to see "one other acquaintance of a sort, Simonov, a former classmate." If the narrator is attracted to the officer for his strength and the visibility of his uniform, he is attracted to Simonov for even more interesting qualities: "a certain measure of independence of character and even honesty."[37] Simonov is arranging a going-away party for Zverkov, and the narrator talks his way into an invitation that no one wants to extend him. Unexpectedly, Zverkov himself makes some attempt to be gracious. Although the other members of the party are not an eager audience to the narrator's role of old school chum and fellow gallant, they are at least more accessible than the officer and somewhat more willing to play along. However, the narrator's loathing for himself and the entire situation eventually breaks down all semblances of accord. After insults, recriminations, and too much to drink, he begins stomping up and down the room while the others try to ignore him. He demonstrates his integrity by his "silence," but he cannot simply go because departure would mean relinquishing the audience before whom he must display his superiority and contempt. The episode ends when his audience walks out on him.

At the end of Part One, the Underground Man says that one reason for writing down these episodes from his past is to be able to judge himself better and to enhance his style.[38] Throughout the polemic, though, he has argued against rational judgments and the possibility of progress. In principle he has implied that style is the man; in his performance he has demonstrated the principle; but in practice he has never accepted the fatalistic limitations of the formula. The Underground Man's solution to the failure of one role or style is the adoption of another, with the

37. *Ibid.*, 57.
38. *Ibid.*, 39.

unstated hope that a new persona will constitute a new identity. So as he follows his retreating audience to the brothel, he fantasizes a role in which he wins a spectacular revenge against Zverkov. Then he admits the fantasy is taken from Pushkin and Lermontov. This is not the kind of better judgment he has promised himself, and the fantasy enhances his style only insofar as the *imaginary* Zverkov cannot now ignore the narrator's act. As the Underground Man pursues his audience in quest of an identity, it becomes clear that he can never change. He can only hope to win a more submissive witness, a better community—like the gentlemen of the polemic who are held to silence, or Lisa the prostitute. As projections of himself, these audiences are neither liberating nor hopeful.

Initially, Lisa is the narrator's most suitable confessor. Young, inexperienced, submissive by profession, and a natural victim, she inspires him to "expound my cherished *little ideas* that I had nurtured in my corner. Suddenly something caught fire in me, a kind of goal 'appeared.'" The Underground Man goes on to celebrate the standard pieties about the community of love and marriage with a fervor that would have embarrassed Moll Flanders and that does not fool Lisa a bit. "'How you . . . just like out of a book,' she says, and something that seemed derisive sounded in her voice again." But he goes on, and the intensity of his performance and obvious pain eventually crushes her. In accepting all of the loathing and defeat he projects onto her, she accepts in effect his definition of the kind of audience she should play to his role of free, enlightened compassion. She responds to his "intimacy" with a very touching confessional gesture of her own, when she shows him her love letter from a medical student.[39]

The Underground Man is aware of Lisa's suffering; he is even troubled by it and eager to escape her. Nevertheless, his first act the following day involves perhaps his most blatant self-deception about the ways in which the conventions he relies on to present himself, reveal instead of obscure the nature of his blinding needs.

39. *Ibid.*, 88, 94, 101.

Apparently inspired by his success with Lisa, he composes an apology to Simonov for his behavior at the party.

> To this day I recall with pleasure the truly gentlemanly, good-natured, sincere tone of my letter. Cleverly and nobly, and what's more important, without wasting a single word, I took the blame for everything. I justified myself, "If I may still be allowed to justify myself," by the fact that I was totally unaccustomed to drink, that I had become drunk with the first jigger. . . . I was particularly pleased by that "certain lightness," verging on nonchalance (quite proper, however), that was suddenly reflected in my pen and, better than any possible excuses, immediately let them know that I looked "upon all that mess of the day before" in a rather detached way; that I wasn't at all, not in the least struck down dead on the spot as you, gentlemen, probably think, but on the contrary I looked on it just as a gentleman who is filled with calm self-respect ought to look on it. "The truth, they say, doesn't hurt an honest man."
>
> "There's even some sort of playfulness befitting a marquis," I chortled, rereading the note.[40]

The truth that may not hurt an honest man is devastating to such a self-deceiver, for the truth seems to be that Simonov would be able to see through the cavalier poses as easily as the reader does. The Simonov the Underground Man addresses is as much a fiction as the gentlemen he is compelled to address again, and both are projections, not of the narrator's real identity, but of the false self-image he would impose on a world in which he can play marquis.

When the Underground Man is confronted by someone who sees him for what he is, he becomes brutally cynical, impotent, and terrifying. For when Lisa comes in response to his own invitation and professes her love, he screams: "And I'll also never forgive *you* for the things that I am confessing to you now! Yes—

40. *Ibid.*, 103.

you, you alone will have to answer for all this." He cannot bear that she understands and loves him; he is outraged that their roles have been reversed and she is now the "heroine." He tries to drive her away by paying her off, but then he chases after her because it is as difficult for him to relinquish any audience as it is for him to fire Apollon, who is the easy victor in the power games the Underground Man tries to play.[41]

Throughout this final episode the Underground Man's greatest fear is not that he is misunderstood, but understood too well. Yet as he tries to bring his notes to a close, he once again steps back from himself and delivers on behalf of the gentlemen another perfect critique of his own performance, calling it "self-centered nastiness" and condemning his estrangement from "living life." For a moment he seems to know exactly who he is and is able to preserve his freedom by repudiating the gentlemen once again.

> "Speak for yourself," you will say, "and your miserable life in the underground, but don't you dare say 'we all.' " Just a minute, gentlemen, after all, I am not trying to exonerate myself with that *we-allness*. As far as I in particular am concerned, I only carried out in my life to the extreme what you didn't dare carry out even halfway, and, to top it all, you took your cowardice for common sense, deceiving yourselves, and you were comforted by it. So that I, if you please, turn out to be still more "alive" than you. Take a closer look! After all, we don't even know exactly where this "living" lives nowadays, and what sort of thing it is, what it's called? . . . We even find it hard to be men—men with real *individual* bodies and blood; we are ashamed of it. . . . Soon we'll think up a way to be born somehow from ideas. But enough; I don't want to write "from the Underground" any more.[42]

After he attacks the rationalists' cowardice and reaffirms his own commitment to experience, the Underground Man's final words

41. *Ibid.*, 117, 119.
42. *Ibid.*, 124–25.

are almost too pat in their irony. No one is more oppressed by real individuality than he is, no one labors more anxiously to be born from his ideas, and he cannot stop writing. At a sudden and obvious distance from the narrator, the editor himself addresses the reader with uninsistent assurance to say that he and the reader both understand the Underground Man so well that almost nothing more need be said: "The 'notes' of this paradoxicalist do not end here, however. He could not resist, and continued on. But it seems to us that we might as well stop here."

The Underground Man understands confession well enough to have condemned Rousseau for lying to his audience out of vanity, and he has embarked on his own confession, he says at the end of Part One, "to make a test to find out: is it possible to be completely open with one's own self at least, and not be afraid of the whole truth?"[43] It may be possible, but in his case the final answers are no. The reminiscences of Part Two contain a relentless apology for his own superiority in the face of overwhelming evidence to the contrary; and because he has no real audience, he is apologizing only to himself. Confessions find their end in community; apologies like the Underground Man's are endless. He has no apparent future but the rehearsal of his past.

There is, of course, another way to evaluate the open-endedness of *Notes from Underground*, and Reed Merrill makes the case intelligently. "The fact that his diatribe is cut off by the editor does not in any sense weaken the case of the Underground Man but only proves that his argument is beyond resolution."[44] This is certainly true of his argument, but his argument is not the only thing at stake. Dostoevsky places the polemic first so that the narrator's case can have its full effect, but Dostoevsky does not locate his narrator's identity in his argument alone. Neither does

43. *Ibid.*, 38.

44. Reed Merrill, "The Mistaken Endeavor: Dostoevsky's *Notes from Underground*," *Modern Fiction Studies*, XVIII (Winter, 1972–73), 515. A more enlightening study of the novel's irresolution is made by M. M. Bakhtin, "Monologue Speech of the Hero, and Narrative Discourse in the Stories of Dostoevsky—*Notes from Underground*," trans. Richard Balthazar, reprinted in Dostoevsky, *Notes from Underground*, 203–16.

the Underground Man himself: this is exactly the kind of prescriptive mentality for which he attacks the rationalists. No confessor, no community could alleviate totally the Underground Man's terrible pain; but in a sympathetic community that subscribes to the values of suffering, experience, and self-knowledge, the Underground Man can be honored for his courage and for the fierceness of his resistance to dehumanizing ideas. To this extent, he is not beyond some kind of solace and confirmation. But he refuses to play along, to accept what he is asking for. He hides himself behind his anonymity, condemns even the possibility of a sympathetic audience, and violates at every brilliant turn the confession he chooses to make. He is exactly right, with a terrible irony, about having no readers. As we read the editor's final note and share its understanding, we leave the narrator as abruptly as Simonov left him at the party—all by himself.

"Call me Ishmael," Ishmael says as simply as he can.[45] He does not say, "My name is Ishmael," because Ishmael is clearly not his given name. And he cannot say, "I am Ishmael," because, by beginning his confession, he is no longer simply the outsider, and the identity he is trying to realize after his symbolic death and rebirth is still in question, in process.[46] Moreover, "Call me Ishmael" is both an imperative and a friendly request: a characteristic

45. My reading of *Moby-Dick* has been formed by four critics in particular: Walter E. Bezanson, "*Moby-Dick*: Work of Art," in Tyrus Hillway and Luther S. Mansfield (eds.), *Moby-Dick: Centennial Essays* (Dallas: Southern Methodist University Press, 1953), 30–58; Paul Brodtkorb, Jr., *Ishmael's White World* (New Haven, Conn.: Yale University Press, 1965); Charles Feidelson, Jr., *Symbolism and American Literature* (Chicago: University of Chicago Press, 1953); and Leslie A. Fiedler, *Love and Death in the American Novel* (Cleveland: World, 1962). Bezanson is particularly good on the novel's styles; Brodtkorb on Ishmael's consistency; Feidelson on symbolism and process; Fiedler on Queequeg and the marriage theme.

46. Everyone has something to say about the novel's opening lines. See, for instance, Goldknopf, *Life of the Novel*, 30–31. My own reading is closest to that of Warner Berthoff, *The Example of Melville* (Princeton, N.J.: Princeton University Press, 1962), 117–20. Brodtkorb's reading is more skeptical; see *Ishmael's White World*, 123. Also see Robert Zoellner, *The Salt-Sea Mastodon* (Berkeley: University of California Press, 1973), 119.

mixture of the moods and tones Ishmael will use throughout his confession to involve the reader, his confessor, in the project of identifying himself and creating the community in which he can have his new life. Like Augustine and Rousseau, Ishmael writes from the midst of the crisis he is trying to resolve by making a confession; and as Roy Harvey Pearce says, he writes to "urge our assent to his utter freedom to adduce material from whatever quarter he wishes and to write from various points of view and in various forms, just so he may understand what has happened to him, just so he may create himself, or at least the possibility of himself."[47] Immediately urging our assent to his identity, he increases his chances of succeeding in his self-creation because our assent is a confirmation that does not diminish his freedom. Moreover, naming him, we name ourselves as part of the community within which Ishmael wants to establish his freedom. "Call me Ishmael" is, perhaps, the most purely confessional line in our literature, for it so clearly evokes its response.

"Call me Ishmael," is also an essentially hopeful line, looking toward the future, and it leads immediately into a serious definition of the reader, the community Ishmael wants. Although his tone is breezy and confident, Ishmael's attitude toward his own experience virtually assumes that we, too, have considered suicide as naturally as he has; that we, too, share his feelings about the ocean and meditation. He says, still in his first paragraph, "If they but knew it, almost all men in their degree, some time or other, cherish very nearly the same feelings towards the ocean with me." He goes on to say, "As every one knows, meditation and water are wedded for ever." His invitation is broad, but his propositions are not exactly self-evident; each reader who assents to them is already being singled out from "almost all men" and the generous "every one." This reader is also being a little misled, for Ishmael's feelings toward the ocean are as ambivalent as the ocean's own natural and symbolic properties. If the ocean is both the field of adventure and the ground of serious, metaphysical speculation—

47. Roy Harvey Pearce, *The Continuity of American Poetry* (Princeton, N.J.: Princeton University Press, 1967), 179.

"the image of the ungraspable phantom of life"—it is also the burial plot of the *Pequod* and the harbor of Moby Dick. Moreover, the kind of speculation the ocean sponsors demands the courage to withstand infinitude, irresolution, and the endless uncertainty of process, as Ishmael explains in his apostrophe to Bulkington in Chapter 23.[48]

> Know ye, now, Bulkington? Glimpses do ye seem to see of that mortally intolerable truth; that all deep, earnest thinking is but the intrepid effort of the soul to keep the open independence of her sea; while the wildest winds of heaven and earth conspire to cast her on the treacherous, slavish shore?
>
> But as in landlessness alone resides the highest truth, shoreless, indefinite as God—so, better is it to perish in that howling infinite, than be ingloriously dashed upon the lee, even if that were safety! For worm-like, then, oh! who would craven crawl to land! Terrors of the terrible! is all this agony so vain?

Yet even without the dangers of the lee shore, there is an equal danger of annihilation, which oceanic reverie can produce in "romantic, melancholy, absent-minded young men," whom Ishmael calls "Platonists" and "Pantheists" and who lose their identities over "Descartesian vortices."

> But lulled into such an opium-like listlessness of vacant, unconscious reverie is this absent-minded youth by the blending cadence of waves with thoughts, that at last he loses his identity; takes the mystic ocean at his feet for the visible image of that deep, blue, bottomless soul, pervading mankind and nature; and every strange, half-seen, gliding, beautiful thing that eludes him; every dimly-discovered, uprising fin of some undiscernible form, seems to him the embodiment of those elusive thoughts that only people the soul by continually flitting through it. In this enchanted mood, thy spirit ebbs away to whence

48. Herman Melville, *Moby-Dick*, ed. Harrison Hayford and Hershell Parker (New York: W. W. Norton, 1967), 12, 13, 14.

> it came; becomes diffused through time and space: like Wickliff's sprinkled Pantheistic ashes, forming at last a part of every shore the round globe over.[49]

Ishmael issues this warning, for he too had once felt himself "losing all consciousness; at last my soul went out of my body." And Pip's madness is caused when he falls overboard and experiences such "intense concentration of self in the middle of such a heartless immensity" that it annihilates his reason.[50]

Against this kind of annihilation, Ishmael later offers a metaphor of self-possession in which the land is not a "treacherous, slavish shore" but an island. "Consider all this; and then turn to this green, gentle, and most docile earth; consider them both, the sea and the land; and do you not find a strange analogy to something in yourself? For as this appalling ocean surrounds the verdant land, so in the soul of man there lies one insular Tahiti, full of peace and joy, but encompassed by all the horrors of the half known life. God keep thee! Push out off from that isle, thou canst never return!" Here, as in his opening paragraphs, Ishmael uses the same mixture of tones in addressing his audience directly. He orders, asks, persuades us to accept his conceit, and exhorts us, for our own good, to keep his counsel. Later, he reaffirms this ideal of self-possession in Chapter 87, "The Grand Armada," in which his metaphor is a "lake" of whales in the middle of the ocean—a lake where cows and calves live a familial life and "young Leviathans" have their "amours in the deep."[51]

These metaphors of self-possession, however, are not all Ishmael needs to be himself, as the form of his confession implies. He is too complex a character to be so simply self-contained; what has happened to him to make him Ishmael, "*another orphan*," is too enormous to be resolved in these moments of peace. "Explain myself I must," he says and his full explanation entails a very great deal, an almost unprecedented range of experiences that, listed, sound something like St. Paul's famous catalog of the

49. *Ibid.*, 97–98, 140.
50. *Ibid.*, 241, 347.
51. *Ibid.*, 236, 324–26.

events that befell him.[52] For Ishmael's confession is an account of his three conversionary experiences, an heroic romance of Ahab, a study of the business and adventure of whaling, a novelistic record of the manners of whalers, the story of his improbable friendship with Queequeg, and the anatomy of cetology that he uses to investigate the nature of reality and the mysteries of good and evil. But his own reality and the credibility of his narrative depend primarily on two things: that the great sperm whale, however unprecedented and incomprehensible to most men, is real; and that the confessional audience accept that reality as a correlative of Ishmael's own. So the cetology that fills his confession is not the encyclopedic compulsion of a funny scholar. It is Ishmael's mode of apology, the rhetorical instrument he uses to define his audience and win the confirmation he needs against the terrible, indeterminate fluidity of the "I" that he sees when he gazes into the endless ocean.[53]

To the community he needs, Ishmael ultimately attributes an extraordinary freedom. The identity he is trying to realize is like the book he is trying to write, and he says of both of them: "For small erections may be finished by their first architects; grand ones, true ones, even leave the copestone to posterity. God keep me from ever completing anything. This whole book is but a draught—nay, but the draught of a draught. Oh, Time, Strength, Cash, and Patience!"[54] In wishing never to complete anything, Ishmael wants for himself the "open independence" of process he apotheosizes in Bulkington; yet this statement also represents Ishmael's recognition that he cannot complete his own life in himself. So we, his posterity and confessor, are left to complete the draught of his book and to complement his identity as we confirm it; and to do this, we are given the kind of individual independence that only the freest confessional writers bestow on their confessors. Augustine can do it only after insisting on God's

52. *Ibid.*, 163; 2 Cor., 11:23–28. Many of Paul's epistles are also, obviously, confessional in their intention and structure.

53. See Zoellner, *Salt-Sea Mastodon*, Chap. 7.

54. Melville, *Moby Dick*, 128–29.

primacy and the community's constitution in charity; Rousseau cannot do it at all; and the Underground Man fears the freedom of his confessors desperately. But Ishmael wants such freedom for himself, and he has the courage to ask of his confessors two things at once: that we "own" the whale as he does, reflecting and confirming him; and that we also be "other," not so much his image as his complement. It is in his idea of complementarity that Ishmael proposes his idea of community, and it is in his relationship with Queequeg that he embodies this ideal.

If Queequeg is nothing else, he is "other." Ishmael is a white, Presbyterian schoolmaster who has never been whaling; Queequeg is a tattooed cannibal, a merchant of shrunken heads, and an expert harpooner. They meet in a real and symbolic marriage bed; and in the morning grip of Queequeg's "bridegroom clasp," Ishmael recalls an apparently analogous experience from childhood that represents for him the terrors the "other" can hold. Waking from a nightmare doze, he felt the presence in his room of a "nameless, unimaginable, silent form or phantom" that placed a "supernatural hand" in his. With Queequeg, however, this analogy does not apply. If, as Ishmael remarks later on, "the invisible spheres were formed in fright," "in many of its aspects this visible world seems formed in love"; and so it is with Queequeg, whose love is not only complementary but redeeming.[55] Ishmael says:

> I began to be sensible of strange feelings. I felt a melting in me. No more my splintered heart and maddened hand were turned against the wolfish world. This soothing savage had redeemed it. There he sat, his very indifference speaking a nature in which there lurked no civilized hypocrysies and bland deceits. Wild he was; a very sight of sights to see; yet I began to feel myself mysteriously drawn toward him. And those same things that would have repelled most others, they were the very magnets that thus drew me. I'll try a pagan friend, thought I, since Christian kindness has proved but hollow courtesy. . . . He seemed to take to me quite as naturally

55. *Ibid.*, 33, 169.

> and unbiddenly as I to him; and when our smoke was over, he pressed his forehead against mine, clasped me round the waist, and said that henceforth we were married; meaning, in his country's phrase, that we were bosom friends; he would gladly die for me, if need should be. In a countryman, this sudden flame of friendship would have seemed far too premature, a thing to be much distrusted; but in this simple savage those old rules would not apply.[56]

Queequeg complements Ishmael in archetypal ways: he is nature to Ishmael's civilization and embodies a wholeness of being in contrast to the divided restlessness of Ishmael's mind. "And yet he seemed entirely at his ease; preserving the utmost serenity; content with his own companionship; always equal to himself. Surely this was a touch of fine philosophy." After Queequeg has somersaulted a mimicking bumpkin and then dived to his rescue a moment later, Ishmael exclaims, "Was there ever such unconsciousness?"[57]

Yet Queequeg is not simply the intellectual's cartoon of the natural man. Ishmael's confession contains the portraits of many other characters who embody various degrees of natural "unconsciousness" and great physical skill: the other harpooners, Fedallah, the ship's carpenter, and even, to some extent, Stubb. Queequeg is also a prince, with civil graces and an innate delicacy; in certain ways, he represents experience to Ishmael's innocence. But perhaps most important of all, Ishmael also sees Queequeg as displaced, a "creature in the transition state," like himself. Queequeg is a religious man as well, whose worship inspires in Ishmael his first conversion; for without too strenuous an examination of conscience, Ishmael can bring himself to worship Queequeg's idol, Yojo. Ishmael's idolatry confirms the force of Queequeg's redemptive love and turns Ishmael away from the inadequate conventions of the Christian community. But it also turns him outward, rather than back into himself, toward a larger community

56. *Ibid.*, 53.
57. *Ibid.*, 52, 61.

in universal brotherhood and a realm of experience that conventional ideas do not comprehend. Ishmael signals his openness to this new world of experience when he goes by himself to select the ship on which they will sail together; he expresses his new credo when he introduces Queequeg to the skeptical, "orthodox" Peleg and Bildad as an equal member in "the great and everlasting First Congregation of this whole worshipping world; we all belong to that; only some of us cherish some queer crochets noways touching the grand belief; in *that* we all join hands."[58]

Ishmael's first conversion has its irony, however, for it prepares him for his second conversion, which is into a far less open congregation. This second conversion takes place in Chapter 36, which follows immediately Ishmael's warning in Chapter 35 that individual identity can be annihilated by too much isolated speculation. The lesson of Chapter 36 is that identity can also be annihilated by totalitarian communities in which individuals have no individuality at all. From his commanding position on the quarter-deck itself, Ahab makes the overwhelming speech that subsumes the will of the entire crew and commits it to Ahab's heroic idea of himself and his revenge, which entails a commitment to death as the ultimate achievement and freedom. For all its democratic variety of types and its trappings of hierarchy in Chapters 26 and 27, the *Pequod* is not so much a modern democracy or feudal principality as it is a fascist state.[59] Ishmael later says, "They were one man, not thirty." And the ceremony that Ahab improvises to confirm the crew's mass conversion enacts the political reorganization of the Pequod in religious terms that are equally totalitarian. Quaker Ahab refers to himself as the Pope, he calls his pagan harpooners "my sweet cardinals," and he demotes the three mates

58. *Ibid.*, 34, 83.

59. See Susan Sontag, "Fascinating Fascism," *New York Review of Books*, February 6, 1975, pp. 23–30. Charles Olson touches on this point in *Call Me Ishmael* (New York: Reynal and Hitchcock, 1947), 64–65. For another opinion, see Henry Nash Smith, "The Image of Society in *Moby-Dick*," in Hillway and Mansfield (eds.), *Moby-Dick: Centennial Essays*, 59–75.

into being cup-bearers to the "cardinals," who drink from the cups of their harpoons a pledge to Moby Dick's death.[60]

Only Starbuck objects, but he is doomed to fail, for he is the impotent voice of reasonableness, conventional decency, and common moral sense. If Ishmael himself were a more conventional character, he would be something like Starbuck—a figure of the common reader, objecting to this madness. But Ishmael saves himself symbolically by losing himself, and he gains from this loss an understanding of community that eventually informs his confession. In Chapter 41, which follows the midnight party on the forecastle from which Ishmael and Queequeg are conspicuously absent, Ishmael says: "I, Ishmael, was one of that crew; my shouts had gone up with the rest; my oath had been welded with theirs; and stronger I shouted, and more did I hammer and clinch my oath, because of the dread in my soul. A wild, mystical, sympathetical feeling was in me; Ahab's quenchless feud seemed mine. With greedy ears I learned the history of that murderous monster against whom I and all the others had taken our oaths of violence and revenge."[61]

Ishmael's "greedy ears" are his first scholarly apparatus. From the more experienced whalemen he begins to hear the legends and superstitions that define Moby Dick, but he also begins to realize that the great sperm whale is real. This realization is what saves him from drowning completely in the "wild, mystical, sympathetical feeling" he has for Ahab, who identifies himself in terms of Moby Dick. Ishmael comes to identify himself in terms of the whole species of great sperm whales, but before the chapter ends, he has begun to distance himself from this destructive community by defining its essential speciousness and by apologizing for his mistake in entering it.

> Here, then, was this grey-headed, ungodly old man, chasing with curses a Job's whale round the world, at

60. Melville, *Moby-Dick*, 454, 146.
61. *Ibid.*, 155

> the head of a crew, too, chiefly made up of mongrel renegades, and castaways, and cannibals—morally enfeebled also, by the incompetence of mere unaided virtue or right-mindedness in Starbuck, the invulnerable jollity of indifference and recklessness in Stubb, and the pervading mediocrity of Flask. Such a crew, so officered, seemed specially picked and packed by some infernal fatality to help him to his monomaniac revenge. . . . all this to explain, would be to dive deeper than Ishmael can go. . . . Who does not feel the irresistible arm drag? What skiff in tow of a seventy-four can stand still? For one, I gave myself up to the abandonment of the time and the place; but while yet all a-rush to encounter the whale, could see naught in that brute but the deadliest ill.[62]

These are strong words from the man who loves Queequeg's difference and who is something of a renegade himself, but they also show how seriously Ishmael takes the ideal and experience of community, how resistant he is to its inadequate forms.

At the end of Chapter 41, Ishmael does his famous disappearing act from the narrative. He continues to be audible as the narrative voice, but he is rarely visible as a participating member of the crew. Ishmael is, as he has been called, a loose fish; and the critical community has filled its own Heidelberg tun with explanations that try to fasten him to conventional expectations. Many of these explanations are the efforts of twentieth-century readers to make a nineteenth-century narrator their contemporary. Nonetheless, if we consider *Moby-Dick* Ishmael's confession, we can provide a few rationalizations for his behavior. Ishmael disappears from the narrative when he relinquishes his personal identity to the group identity of the crew; as no more than an ordinary seaman, he has no special role to play in the pursuit of Moby Dick. He uses this time of invisibility to anatomize the whale, in quest of an understanding of himself and "reality," in trying out the meaning

62. *Ibid.*, 162–63.

of his third conversion, which has turned him away from the *Pequod* and toward the community he must create in order to repossess himself as Ishmael.

In their own ways, Ahab and Ishmael both take liberties with order. Ishmael takes the liberties he does because he has to realize himself under extraordinary circumstances. There are no conventions for self-realization, just as there are no conventions for an anatomy of cetology. And however firmly we may believe in organic form, we have to admit that the order of *Moby-Dick* and of Ishmael's confession often seems insouciant. There are significant clusters of chapters, the carefully orchestrated series of gams, and finally the great sequence of the three-day chase, which resolves a number of things, but not Ishmael's survival and his need to confess. For his confession Ishmael wants no more imposition of system than the Underground Man does. To realize himself, he needs the freedom that his own account of himself enacts, and he exercises this freedom in presenting to us the worked-up treatment of the whale. He also exercises it in his treatment of other characters. Here, Ishmael commits his sins of omniscience. Yet when he introduces us to the mind of Ahab or Starbuck, he is doing no more than he does when he takes us into the heads of the various whales: trying to extend the sympathy, and to exercise the imagination, necessary to understand himself in the "other." And when he does resurface into the narrative action, he does so to raise explicitly the issues that are fundamental to the confession he has been making through the cetological materials.

In Chapter 96, for instance, Ishmael spells out the close relationship between personal annihilation in isolated reverie and the loss of self that is possible in a false, destructive community. With the tiller in his hand, Ishmael is drowsy again, but not from gazing into his own image in the deep; he has been looking into the *Pequod's* hold, onto a scene that is a diabolic image of Ahab's totalitarianism. Ishmael saves himself and the whole crew when he jerks awake and becomes responsible again.

In the other episodes in which he reappears, Ishmael is more positive about the benefits a proper community can have, and many of these scenes involve Queequeg. In Chapter 47, as he and Queequeg are weaving a sword mat, Ishmael draws from their cooperation a conceit about complementarity. The warp seems like necessity, Ishmael's shuttle represents his own free will, and Queequeg's sword is the agency of chance—"no wise incompatible—all interweavingly worked together." Not long after, Ishmael is swamped for the first time and he recapitulates his first conversion by thinking of his rescue as a rebirth that inspires him to draw his will and to make the omnicompetent Queequeg his "lawyer, executor, and legatee." In Chapter 72, in which the monkey-rope attaches Ishmael to Queequeg like an "elongated Siamese ligature," Ishmael sees that even with Queequeg community brings its responsibility. "I seemed distinctly to perceive that my own individuality was not merged in a joint stock company of two: that my free will had received a mortal wound; and that another's mistake or misfortune might plunge innocent me into unmerited disaster or death."[63] As in Chapter 47, "The Mat-Maker," Ishmael identifies himself with "free will" and realizes that even in the best of company his free will has its limits. Still, he goes on to disqualify the selfishness of his words when he recognizes that his relationship with Queequeg is representative of all human interdependence and that his freedom contains the power to save Queequeg from the sharks. The insight is important to Ishmael because he is usually so passive and Queequeg is the one to the rescue, but complementarity works both ways: Queequeg's tomahawk is a peace pipe, and the coffin Ishmael helps him build eventually becomes Ishmael's life buoy.

Perhaps the most significant reappearance Ishmael makes is in Chapter 94, which follows immediately the chapter in which Pip goes mad. The chapter title, "A Squeeze of the Hand," echoes Ishmael's words about "the great and ever-lasting First Congregation of the whole worshipping world . . . in *that* we all join hands"; and it presents as powerful an image of active community as Augustine presents in the passage where "comrades' love" was

63. *Ibid.*, 185, 196, 271.

"like fuel to set our minds ablaze and to make but one out of many."[64] Ishmael says:

> I declare to you, that for the time I lived as in a musky meadow; I forgot all about our horrible oath; in that inexpressible sperm, I washed my hands and my heart of it; I almost began to credit that old Paracelsan superstition that sperm is of rare virtue in allaying the heat of anger: while bathing in that bath, I felt divinely free from all ill-will, or petulance, or malice, of any sort whatsoever.
>
> Squeeze! squeeze! squeeze! all the morning long; I squeezed that sperm till I myself almost melted into it; I squeezed that sperm till a strange sort of insanity came over me; and I found myself unwittingly squeezing my co-laborers' hands in it, mistaking their hands for the gentle globules. Such an abounding, affectionate, friendly, loving feeling did this vocation beget; that at last I was continually squeezing their hands, and looking up into their eyes sentimentally; as much to say,—Oh! my dear fellow beings, why should we longer cherish any social acerbities, or know the slightest ill-humor or envy! Come; let us squeeze hands all round; nay, let us all squeeze ourselves into each other; let us squeeze into the very milk and sperm of kindness.
>
> Would that I could keep squeezing that sperm for ever! For now, since by many prolonged, repeated experiences, I have perceived in all cases man must eventually lower, or at least shift, his conceit of attainable felicity; not placing it anywhere in the intellect or fancy; but in the wife, the heart, the bed, the table, the saddle, the fire-side, the country; now that I have perceived all this, I am ready to squeeze case eternally. In visions of the night, I saw long rows of angels in paradise, each with his hands in a jar of spermaceti.[65]

Ishmael's wishes go unfulfilled: he cannot continue to squeeze

64. *Ibid.*, 83.
65. *Ibid.*, 348–49.

sperm, and he does not seem to enjoy a wife and fireside. However, he does overcome his desire to lose himself completely in either isolation or a false community; for the community his confession creates, exists within his audience's acceptance of the whale's reality, which he insists upon. As he writes his confession, Ishmael grows. He does not lose himself in the project but extends himself through it and achieves a sense of himself that he never possessed aboard the *Pequod*. His grandiloquence in the following passage is exuberant and funny, but his statement is serious. The great sperm whale, not Moby Dick alone, is his subject and correlative, and its scope determines not only the variety of his methods, but also the comprehensiveness of his own identity.

> One often hears of writers that rise and swell with their subject, though it may seem but an ordinary one. How, then, with me, writing of this Leviathan? Unconsciously my chirography expands into placard capitals. Give me a condor's quill! Give me Vesuvius' crater for an inkstand! Friends, hold my arms! For in the mere act of penning my thoughts on this Leviathan, they weary me, and make me faint with their outreaching comprehensiveness of sweep, as if to include the whole circle of the sciences, and all the generations of whales, and men, and mastodons, past, present, and to come, with all the revolving panoramas of empire on earth, and throughout the whole universe, not excluding its suburbs. Such, and so magnifying, is the virtue of a large and liberal theme! We expand to its bulk. To produce a mighty book, you must choose a mighty theme. No great and enduring volume can ever be written on the flea, though many there be who have tried it.[66]

We, too, expand to its bulk if we hear Ishmael properly, and he is careful to give us his own version of the "strange children" from whom we are to distance ourselves in order to accept the truth of his account. First among these are the other writers on whales. *Moby-Dick* begins with an Etymology and a series of

66. *Ibid.*, 379.

Extracts that suggest how broad the topic of the whale is and how contradictory the previous accounts are. The writers Ishmael scorns are those who have written without ever having seen a whale; he honors Captain Scoresby, who has been alone among them "a real professional harpooner and whaleman." Ishmael also takes to task the graphic artists who have depicted the whale falsely. "The living whale, in his full majesty and significance, is only to be seen at sea in unfathomable waters and even here he is not wholly visible to the eye."[67]

Ishmael's cetology does the usual work of realism, which is to be critical, empirical, corrective; and his authority derives not merely from his dubious, sometimes hilarious scholarship, but primarily from his own experience. He is hostile toward those who would substitute for experience an illusive explanation. "So ignorant are most landsmen of some of the plainest and most palpable wonders of the world, that without some hints touching the plain facts, historical and otherwise, of the fishery, they might scout at Moby Dick as a monstrous fable, or still worse and more detestable, a hideous intolerable allegory." In the metaphysical conceits he yokes, in the morals he draws as easily as Father Mapple does, in the constant play of his mind across the facts he marshals in order to understand or create their value and significance, Ishmael admits to the "linked analogies" between "Nature" and "the human soul of man"; but analogies are not allegories. Analogies are more natural and open, less artful and less definitive than allegories. And for a man who is trying to identify himself in a world whose reality is so fiercely ambivalent and complex, allegories are an evasion. They relinquish the meaning of experience to an extranatural or supernatural order that is too simple and closed. Everything that Ishmael says about the whale is a statement about himself, and he knows that he is not an allegory. "Call me Ishmael." Calling him anything else is denying him, allegorizing him. And allegorists are to Ishmael what rationalists are to the Underground Man: they simplify experience into mere ideas.[68]

67. *Ibid.*, 117, 227–28.

68. *Ibid.*, 177, 264. While Melville was writing *Moby-Dick*, he was also

So Ishmael's attitude toward his cetological material has two complementary aspects. He is both insistently didactic about the facts he presents and absolutely honest about his inability to teach his audience all they have to know. This, again, is a function of the realism of *Moby-Dick*. Instruction, ideas, opinions, symbols, art—none of them can replace experience. If the reader is to complete the book and to confirm and complement Ishmael, he must go whaling himself in order to fully understand what Ishmael has undergone. But as always, Ishmael's imperatives are requests and an honest counsel to his audience of what he believes is beneficial to us, and his words seem to embody three very different gestures. Some of them point his pedagogue's finger at our ignorance; some throw his hands in the air at the impossibility of his task; and some open his arms to invite us into the whale itself.

Ishmael points his finger first in Chapter 24. "As Queequeg and I are now fairly embarked in this business of whaling; and as this business of whaling has somehow come to be regarded among landsmen as a rather unpoetical and disreputable pursuit; therefore, I am all anxiety to convince ye, ye landsmen, of the injustice hereby done to us hunters of whales." He goes on to assure us immediately that we "shall soon be initiated into certain facts hitherto pretty generally unknown." But he leaves the final resolution of the mystery to us. "I promise nothing complete because any human thing supposed to be complete, must for that very reason infallibly be faulty. . . . I am the architect, not the builder." And later he says: "So there is no earthly way of finding out precisely what the whale really looks like. And the only mode in which you can derive even a tolerable idea of his living contour,

---

writing a series of somewhat confessional letters to Nathaniel Hawthorne. Hawthorne and his wife both responded to the novel's "allegories," and Melville responded in a famous letter to Sophia Hawthorne. See *The Letters of Herman Melville*, ed. Merrill R. Davis and William H. Golman (New Haven, Conn.: Yale University Press, 1960), especially 145–46. For reactions to this letter see Newton Arvin, *Herman Melville* (William Sloane Associates, 1950), 165–66; Feidelson, *Symbolism and American Literature*, 176; and Zoellner, *Salt-Sea Mastodon*, 14.

is by going whaling yourself; but by so doing, you run no small risk of being eternally stove and sunk by him. Wherefore, it seems to me you had best not be too fastidious in your curiosity touching this Leviathan."[69]

But the caveat Ishmael issues is a joke and a challenge, a rhetorical come-on. He wants not only to compel our fastidious attention but also to complete the motif of his own conversions by effecting a conversion in us. As Frank McConnell has explained, in the tradition of Quaker confessions especially, it is the speaker's purpose to be so edifying that his listener be converted too. Ishmael begins to work this conversion on the reader as early as Chapter 45, in which he contemns allegories and complains of being called "facetious," to which he responds by saying: "Was not Saul of Tarsus converted from unbelief by a similar fright? I tell you, the sperm whale will stand no nonsense."[70] Because Ishmael realizes that most of his readers will not go whaling, he tries to break through the pasteboard of his own narrative by bringing us, literally, inside the whale. In Chapter 76, after he has taken us into the heads of the right and sperm whales, he exhorts us to settle for ourselves the question of the sperm whale's power.

> Ere quitting, for the nonce, the Sperm Whale's head, I would have you, as a sensible physiologist, simply—particularly remark its front aspect, in all its compacted collectedness. I would have you investigate it now with the sole view of forming to yourself some unexaggerated, intelligent estimate of whatever battering ram power may be lodged there. Here is a vital point; for you must either satisfactorily settle this matter with yourself, or for ever remain an infidel as to one of the most appalling, but not the less true events, perhaps anywhere to be found in all recorded history.[71]

69. *Ibid.*, 98, 118, 228.

70. See Frank D. McConnell, *The Confessional Imagination: A Reading of Wordworth's Prelude* (Baltimore: Johns Hopkins University Press, 1974), 29; Melville, *Moby-Dick*, 179.

71. Melville, *Moby-Dick*, 284.

Ishmael wants from us a response that is free, empirical (as "sensible physiologists"), and intelligent; but if we do not agree with him, we "for ever remain an infidel." "For unless you own the whale, you are but a provincial and sentimentalist in Truth."[72]

This conversionary motif is brought to its climax in the cluster of chapters from Chapter 102 to Chapter 104, in which Ishmael himself enters the full skeleton of a beached sperm whale. He goes about taking scientific measurements. But he does not forget to allude to Jonah, he explains that the people of Tranque have made this skeleton a "grand temple" in which they conduct their worship, and he develops the significance of the skeleton overgrown with tropical verdure: "Life folded Death; Death trellised Life; the grim god wived with youthful Life, and begat him curly-headed glories." All of Ishmael's perspicacity about Nature's ambivalence, his own ideal of a redeeming complementarity, and the history of his own resurrection are epitomized here. He does not deceive himself that a beached skeleton is the real thing—"only on the profound unbounded sea, can the fully invested whale be truly and livingly found out." But in this same chapter he explains how he has expanded "to its bulk" in writing about the great sperm whale. And he ends the chapter quietly with the confidence that the reader has been converted: "In this Afric Temple of the Whale I leave you, reader, and if you be a Nantucketer and a whaleman, you will silently worship there."[73]

Those who remain constitute Ishmael's confessional community, which is something like "the great and everlasting First Congregation of the whole worshipping world," and also like the transitory community of sailors who spent the day squeezing the sacramental spermaceti and one anothers' hands. But there is this important distinction, especially from the sperm-squeezers. Ishmael leaves the reader by himself: he does not wish that we melt into him, or that he remain and melt into us. In writing his confession, he has come to the kind of freedom and self-possession that cure him of his longing for an oceanic annihilation. And the metaphor

72. *Ibid.*, 285–86.
73. *Ibid.*, 374, 375, 378, 379, 381.

for community that emerges is the state of marriage. Ishmael began with Queequeg in a marriage bed; squeezing the sperm, he has his vision of "the wife, the heart, the bed, the table, the saddle, the fire-side, the country"; in Chapter 87, "The Grand Armada," it is his vision of the whale's familiar life that pacifies him; and in king Tranquo's skeletal temple, Ishmael sees the "grim god" of the whale "wived" and begetting "curly-headed glories." As both a metaphor and a real condition, marriage implies stability, "landedness," complementarity, and a fruitful future. In Chapter 132, "The Symphony," which immediately precedes "The Chase—First Day," even Ahab softens for a moment as the beautiful weather makes him think of his wife and son; and Starbuck's plea that they save themselves is a plea to return home: "Away with me! let us fly these deadly waters! let us home! Wife and child, too, are Starbuck's—wife and child of his brotherly, sisterly, playfellow youth; even as thine, sir, are the wife and child of thy loving, longing, paternal old age!"[74] For neither of them, however, is there any future but death. Only Ishmael survives. He is saved on Queequeg's coffin by the fatherly captain of the motherly Rachel *"that in her retracing search after her missing children, only found another orphan."*

This marital metaphor for community domesticates the ideal of complementarity that Ishmael has embodied in his relationship with Queequeg and, perhaps, makes the ideal more accessible, if less exciting, to the reader who has not been whaling with a Queequeg of his own. In either form, this community fulfills Ishmael's confessional intention. In the community he defines, he can be called Ishmael by a reader who has acquired a much deeper sense of what being Ishmael entails; and in this community, there is the kind of freedom Ishmael wants for us as well, so that we may respond to his constant invitations to adduce our own meanings, values, and possibilities. To this extent *Moby-Dick* is an optimistic book. Still, although Ismael's confession informs *Moby-Dick*, that confessional form is neither comprehensive of the novel as a

74. *Ibid.*, 444.

whole nor even finally comprehensive of Ishmael himself, for the confessional act is always a new beginning. Ishmael has defined the community he needs, but he has done so by writing what is only the draft of a draft of a single volume that is to be part of his projected autobiographical study of the great sperm whale and his own identity. He may share with Moll Flanders a belief in the benefits of marriage, but he has not really lowered or shifted his "conceit of attainable felicity"; it still remains in his "intellect" and "fancy," and he is still resisting the lee shore.[75]

Like the Underground Man, Ishmael enacts himself in the act of writing. The crucial difference between them, however, is that Ishmael never denies us, never insists that he be taken only at his word, and he always allows us every perspective on himself and his experience that he can imagine. Ishmael himself never tells us what he thinks of the doubloon; he reports Pip saying, "I look, you look, he looks; we look, ye look, they look." These words are also a metaphor of complementarity and much truer to the meaning of Ishmael's confession and the community it creates than the metaphor of marriage is, because the metaphor of complementary perspectives is more open to the variety of experience. When the Underground Man undercuts himself in the polemic, he does it to keep his gentlemen off balance and to maintain his own superiority. When Ishmael undercuts himself, which he does as naturally as he sermonizes, he does it to demonstrate his own limitations, to expose the limits of art, and to engage the reader in the problem art has in comprehending and articulating experience. Ishmael himself is incomplete; he always regards his body as a blank page for the "poem" he is composing; his book needs unending revision; his community is open to change, disestablishment, reconstitution.[76] If the process is endless, the prospect is not despairing because the premise of Ishmael's identity is couched in the confessional premise of his opening line, "Call me Ishmael," which entails his constant, essential attachment to human community. For a confession, Ishmael's account of his own character accounts

75. *Ibid.*, 349.
76. *Ibid.*, 362, 376.

for a lot of other characters as well. Moll leaves so many of the people in her life unnamed; the Underground Man names relatively more, but neither knows nor loves any of them. Ishmael, however, gives us not only himself, but also Queequeg, Ahab, Starbuck, Stubb, and Pip. In this acknowledgment of "others" lies the greatness of Ishmael himself and the importance of his confession.

II

The Confessor and His Audience

Chapter 4

"Ghostlier Demarcations, Keener Sounds"

O good Horatio, what a wounded name
(Things standing thus unknown) shall live
behind me.
If thou didst ever hold me in thy heart,
Absent thee from felicity awhile,
And in this harsh world draw thy breath in
pain,
To tell my story.

SHAKESPEARE
Hamlet

In *The Nature of Narrative,* Scholes and Kellogg see Rousseau's *Confessions* as a ground of the classical modernist novel and trace modern fiction's formal ambition and stylistic difficulties to Rousseau's belief that his real nature is virtually ineffable. They say: "Two alternatives (not mutually exclusive) lie before the narrative artist who accepts Rousseau's pessimistic distrust of language and the classical virtues. Either the new and typical can be sought at deeper and deeper levels of man's inarticulate nature, with consequently a greater and greater strain on the ability of language to serve as a vehicle for communicating vision, or language itself may become the ultimate material of art, with all human experience contained in some form or another of existing linguistic structures."[1] James Joyce, D. H. Lawrence, Virginia Woolf, and William Faulkner are obvious examples of the narrative artist Scholes and Kellogg have in mind, and each one has tried to define and express in the human nature of their characters an "unhuman" element, or an intrinsic principle of "otherness," which their characters may experience, but of which they can hardly speak. In Lawrence's *The Rainbow* it is the "physiology of matter" that most interests him about the Brangwens. In Woolf, it is Mrs. Dalloway's belief that her identity is dispersed or distributed among things in nature as well as among other people; by the same token, it is also Mrs. Ramsay's belief in the dark wedge at her elemental center. For Addie Bundren, in Faulkner's *As I Lay Dying,* it is the terrific passion that rolls along the earth beneath the vertical empty shapes of language. And for Joyce's Blooms, it is in the large-mannered motions of Joyce's mythy mind that Poldy is, despite himself, a god-the-father and Molly the eternal earth, a mountain of flowers. With what seems like greater and greater prophetic acuity, Joyce, Lawrence, Woolf, and Faulkner have dramatized how hard it is for even couples as fatally bound together as Tom and Lydia Brangwen, the Ramsays, the Bundrens, and the Blooms to talk to each other, since, for most of them, their most definitive experience is accessible in language that only their omniscient narrators command or can bestow on them in virtually unspoken soliloquies. It is difficult to imagine Addie or Molly speaking their very important, single chapters out loud. We read all these characters, listening to them be themselves without quite expressing themselves, in styles of prose that finally manage to be neither raw impression nor conventional speech.

It is interesting, too, that no one among these four fairly representative couples is a figure of the artist; in fact, the figures of the artist in these four novels are given no greater authority than the principal couples. Will Brangwen is only a minor craftsman at best; Lily Briscoe's painting resolves itself without being the full

1. Robert Scholes and Robert Kellogg, *The Nature of Narrative* (London: Oxford University Press, 1968), 158.

resolution of *To the Lighthouse*; Darl Bundren goes mad and is committed to the state asylum; and Stephen Dedalus plays Telemachus to Bloom's Odysseus. The point is that extraordinary consciousness is attributed to ordinary characters who are nonetheless incapable of fully understanding themselves or of being understood by anyone but their creators and the reader. The most typical gesture of self-expression in modernist fiction may be the unfinished sentence Bloom writes with a stick in the sands of the Nausicaa chapter: "I AM A   ." And were Gerty McDowell closer, Bloom might just as well have said to her, "Call me Henry Flower."

As modern novelists have altered the novel to accommodate our changing sense of human nature, we have changed our ideas of what confession is in accepting their belief, which squares with Freud's and Reik's, that the full truth of any expression is in the "other" realm of the unconscious. And we tend to think of the representative narrators of modern "confessional" novels as the natural sons of Rousseau and the Underground Man, for they speak from the midst of crises so intense, from an isolation so unrelieved, that the emphasis of their narratives is on identifying themselves against nature, rather than in the context of human society. Before they can define an audience, or even the possibility of an audience, they have to identify themselves; consequently, the ethical project of apology often goes unrealized or remains latent in the search within the self for any ground of value whatsoever. The umbrella word for narrators such as Jean Paul Sartre's Roquentin, Albert Camus' Mersault, Saul Bellow's Dangling Man, and Ralph Ellison's Invisible Man, among others, is *existentialist*, and Peter M. Axthelm sees them as legitimate heirs of the confessional tradition. Yet novels like *Nausea* and *The Stranger* are not confessions according to the paradigm I have proposed because they are addressed to no confessor, and what I find most interesting about them is that the "disappearance" of the confessor from their narratives suggests how deeply narcissism infects the twentieth century.

There are, however, novels that use a confession and fully acknowledge the speaker's difficulty in making it by emphasizing the active, dramatic role of the confessor. In Theodore Dreiser's *An American Tragedy*, Clyde Griffiths confesses as well as he can to his lawyers Reuben Jephson and Alvin Belknap, and then later he tries to confess to the Reverend Duncan McMillan. In F. Scott Fitzgerald's *The Great Gatsby*, Gatsby makes his confession to Nick Carraway. Moll's confessor, the Underground Man's, and Ishmael's are defined by their confessions and are formally present in the structure of each novel; but these confessors are not, as Jephson and Nick are, characters in the narrative. (The editors of *Moll Flanders* and *Notes from Underground* are not active characters in this sense, either.) Moreover, in *Moll Flanders, Notes from Underground*, and *Moby-Dick*, the whole burden of confession and apology lies on the speaker, whereas in *An American Tragedy* and *The Great Gatsby* much of the apology is shifted to the confessor who shapes the confession he has heard, informs it with the meaning he sees in it, and then presents it to another audience. This extension of the confessor's role seems to be a natural way for a novelist to develop the confession's form and to use it in new ways, but it is not a development we notice if we think of confession only as an act of self-expression that needs no confessor, no community for the speaker to enter.

Moreover, in seeing the confessional form's part in novels like *An American Tragedy* and *The Great Gatsby*, as well as in *Lord Jim* and *Absalom, Absalom!*, we can see in other ways what community can be made to mean, what actual alternative it can provide. Because Moll and Ishmael speak directly to the reader, community, however clearly they define it, remains something of an aesthetic abstraction—a better relationship, but one that exists between a fictional character and a real reader. Because Clyde and Gatsby confess to other characters, the communities they define must contend with the other social orders in which they find themselves and from which they take their sense of possibility. And whatever these possibilities may be, they are determined by the assumptions each of these four novelists has about society and community, the nature of character and identity, and his own sense of what his art and narrative technique make possible. As these novels explore the form of confession and the chances of an individual confession's success or failure, the confessional form itself illuminates or measures the books that contain and use it.

By giving an active role to a confessor like Marlow, who understands Jim in a way Jim does not understand himself, Conrad, for instance, saves Jim from the fate of writing only an incomplete sentence like Bloom's, because Marlow fills in the blank. In doing so, Marlow becomes, as the other confessors do, a figure of the artist; and these confessors, by their attention, fidelity, and compassionate imagination, allow art the possibility of having an efficacious voice against what can otherwise be the isolation and silence of a world of intractable fact. Whatever tragedy these novels recognize, they also recognize the hope even of transcendence in the possibility of recognition from other people. In doing so, they recognize whatever heroism there is in simply talking and listening, and they criticize the failures of courage and imagination that can make talking and listening selfish. So, in these confessors, there is not only a portrait of the artist, but a portrait of the reader too.

Reuben Jephson, Clyde's best confessor, presents Clyde's confession to the jury; but the power of his ability to apologize for Clyde is limited by the circumstances in which Jephson must merely function. As the narrator of *The Great Gatsby,* Nick has more freedom than Jephson, for he creates his own function in the story. Moreover, because he discovers in Gatsby a model of his own romantic hope, he wants to define Gatsby as heroic. Nick, however, seems to forget that Gatsby has made a confession, for what he prizes is Gatsby's self-sufficiency. In translating Gatsby's confession into narrative, Nick tries to emulate that mistaken self-sufficiency in a gorgeous gesture of his own, and he leaves open a number of questions about his ability to see Gatsby or himself clearly. The questions raised by Nick lead to questions about Fitzgerald, about his understanding of the form he has used, perhaps about his own self-confidence as an artist.

Conrad has a greater understanding of the form he has used in *Lord Jim* because he makes Marlow take his story of Jim back to an audience of old friends, the men on the veranda. Conrad's incorporation of this audience allows him to develop explicitly several aspects of Marlow's narrative that Fitzgerald leaves implicit, or unrecognized, in Nick's narrative. Marlow's continual need to talk about Jim to those who will listen indicates that Marlow is making his own confession in order to win confirmation of himself and his ideas about Jim, who has converted Marlow to a different understanding of human nature. Marlow's account of Jim also suggests that the heroic personality needs more than a sense of his own destiny, and more than the mythic elevation Nick gives Gatsby; the hero needs the community's recognition of his heroism, which is why Marlow would persuade the men on the veranda that Jim is "one of us." The "privileged man" to whom Marlow writes the letter describing Jim's death, however, represents the community's skepticism, so he is also a figure of the unconvinced reader. But because Marlow confronts him, admitting to his own need for confirmation and taking a chance Nick avoids, his story seems more honest, more credible, and more complete. Marlow's letter also gives the real reader a freedom he does not have with *The Great Gatsby*.

In *Absalom, Absalom!*, Faulkner's experiment with narrative viewpoints and various audiences surpasses even Conrad's. *Absalom, Absalom!* may be the richest use of the confessional form ever made because it contains several confessions, starting with Sutpen's. Its principal confessors become speakers themselves in trying to explain their involvement in Sutpen's life. Perhaps the most remarkable confession is Quentin Compson's, for he makes it without talking much about himself at all. The response of his roommate and confessor Shreve McCannon—whose name is clearly a pun on the old verb that means both to hear and to make a confession—is equally remarkable, for Shreve himself becomes a narrator and extends the confessional community to authorize the reader's response and participation in an exceptional way. Because he thinks Mr. Compson's explanation of Bon must have been wrong, Shreve imagines with Quentin a better account of Bon's attachment to Henry, to Judith, to Sutpen. As a confessor who is both a figure of the reader and figure of the artist, Shreve encourages us to ask for more, or supply it ourselves.

This kind of "collaboration" between narrators and readers, Warner Berthoff says, is an aspect of all first-person narratives that confirms both the narrators' reality and the readers.' "The mode of first-person narration is essentially a comic mode, in the broadest sense. For the great theme of the comic, in Northrop Frye's words, is precisely 'the integration of society.' "[2] By this standard, confession is surely a comic mode too. In the four novels we examine in the second part of this essay, this comic mode is used in an attempt to redeem tragic experience. Clyde Griffiths is a tragic character; Gatsby is also, and perhaps a tragic hero; Jim and Sutpen are tragic heroes certainly. All of them, however, lack the full measure of self-recognition we expect of the tragic personality. Their confessors try to accommodate this lack, however, and in the apologies they make, their confessors try to redeem them from their tragic isolation by integrating them into a confessional community that honors their sense of their own identity and their attempts to achieve freedom. Comic and tragic are one set of poles for these confessional novels; naturalistic and romantic are another. For confession is also a romantic mode insofar as it values the individual primarily and tries to win for the self a place beyond the determinations of naturalistic circumstance. In this sense, the political orientation of the confession is democratic, and the novels before us deal quite explicitly with one of democracy's essential paradoxes: given the right to equality, the individual who would realize himself fully must often transcend conventional ideas of what *equal* means. The freedom that fosters this kind of aspiration often creates its own kind of personal confusion and loneliness, which naturally inspires the need to make a confession, which in turn calls upon its audience to be equal in a new order.

2. Warner Berthoff, *The Example of Melville* (Princeton, N.J.: Princeton University Press, 1962), 120.

Chapter 5

Clyde and Jephson, Gatsby and Nick

For our time the most effective agent of the moral imagination has been the novel of the last two hundred years. It was never, either aesthetically or morally, a perfect form and its faults and failures can be quickly enumerated. But its greatness and its practical usefulness lay in its unremitting work of involving the reader himself in the moral life, inviting him to put his own motives under examination, suggesting that reality is not as his conventional education has led him to see it. It taught us, as no other genre ever did, the extent of human variety and the value of this variety. It was the literary forms to which the emotions of understanding and forgiveness were indigenous, as if by the definition of the form itself.

LIONEL TRILLING
The Liberal Imagination

Alexis de Tocqueville's insight that envy is natural to a society of equals has a correlative in the maxim that comparisons are invidious. With Clyde and Gatsby, however, comparison is also an almost irresistible impulse. *An American Tragedy* and *The Great Gatsby* were both published in 1925 in an era of official national optimism, and both novels rise from the same great clichés to tell the story of a young man who changes his name as he leaves home and heads East, not West, to escape his history and fashion a destiny for himself. Clyde and Gatsby are both naïve, self-centered, and not very sensitive young men on the make in a society where "making it" is an idiom of both sex and commerce. Like Moll Flanders and the Underground Man, they are clothes-conscious, secretive, and role players. And like many "young men from the provinces," they fall in love with beautiful empty girls of greater wealth and station who come to embody their ideals of success and who unwittingly inspire the two outsiders to become outlaws as well. However, crime does not pay in either novel, and both Clyde and Gatsby die proving that the American dream does not always come true. In their separate visions, of course, the two novels differ radically. Fitzgerald does not see James Gatz as an American tragedy typical of others; he sees him as the Great Gatsby. And while he sees that making it in America can be understood as the social disease Dreiser examines, Fitzgerald also sees Gatsby's aspirations as an aspect of the national mythopoeia. Despite the differences between Dreiser's naturalism and Fitzgerald's romanticism, both writers use the confession as their protagonists' last chance to define their identities, to redeem themselves from their failures in a world hostile to their aspirations. Because neither Clyde nor Gatsby makes a confession as full or as explicit as Moll's or Ishmael's, the meaning of their confessions is imparted through their confessors' sympathy and mediation. In Reuben Jephson and Nick Carraway reside the possibilities of freedom and community.

Clyde's first attempt to make a deliberate confession comes when he takes the stand at his trial. A confession of the extenuating circumstances of his life is his only chance of countering the prosecution's overwhelming case.[1] "I was born in Grand Rapids,

1. Robert Penn Warren argues that one of the principal themes of *An American Tragedy* is the theme of identity. See his *Homage to Theodore Dreiser* (New York: Random House, 1971), 124–25. Two other studies of the identity theme are Lauriat Lane, Jr., "The Double in *An American Tragedy*," *Modern Fiction Studies*, XII (Summer, 1966), 213–20, and Julian Markels, "Dreiser and the Plotting of Inarticulate Experience," *Massachusetts Review*, II (Spring, 1961). 1–48.

Michigan," he begins, but he cannot go very far on his own and his voice fades out in the ellipsis at the end of Chapter 23.[2] Clyde is, to say the least, confused about who he is. His three different aliases have made no difference in his life (as aliases have for Moll and Gatsby); the entire Bridgeburg community thinks of him as a Griffiths of Lycurgus, which Clyde would like to be but knows he is not; and he has earlier defended himself to Alvin Belknap, the older of his lawyers, on the grounds that his plan to murder Roberta was inspired by a newspaper account of a similiar crime, which in Clyde's mind mitigates his own responsibility. Unlike Julien Sorel, in roughly similar circumstances, Clyde does not have the character or self-possession to make a defiant admission of his guilt, which would also constitute an act of self-definition. Clyde has always been alone but has lacked Julien's imagination to create a sense of his own independence, so he has always adapted himself to a role, someone else's expectation of him, a social convention. Moreover, he has never had any confidants except his bellboy friends, who taught him little more than how to dress and drink. He cannot tell Sondra what he has done for her; the Griffiths of Lycurgus have repudiated him; and even his mother, despite her love and faith, is ultimately cut off from him by "an unsurmountable wall or impenetrable barrier . . . built by the lack of understanding."[3]

Clyde does receive some sympathy and understanding from his lawyers. Belknap himself, for instance, once impregnated a girl he did not want to marry. But even their sympathy and their power as confessors are undermined for several reasons. They do not quite believe Clyde's story and do not identify with him. In his confusion Clyde does not trust them completely because he knows that the jury, not his lawyers, will ultimately judge him. And Clyde's case is being used by District Attorney Orville Mason to further his own political career. Nonetheless, his lawyers do their best to save Clyde; and from what he has told them about himself, Jephson, especially, devises a defense. This defense is based

2. Theodore Dreiser, *An American Tragedy* (Cleveland: World, 1962), 725.
3. *Ibid.*, 643, 866.

on a lie that they think is necessary to develop a more important truth. The lie is, in the honorific sense of the term, a "fiction" by which Jephson attempts to revaluate the facts and to extend the court's inquiry beyond the meaning of Clyde's crime, which is clear to everyone, into an examination of his identity.

At the beginning of Chapter 24, Jephson intervenes to assume control of Clyde's confession in order to make it as convincing as possible. Jephson's fiction is less lofty and extensive than the one Nick Carraway will erect over Gatsby. For with a necessary irony, the identity Jephson wants to give Clyde initially is quite similar to the identity the prosecution attributes to him too: a young man of good family, educational advantages, and prosperity, which his clothes and "travel" indicate. Jephson coaches Clyde to play a role of self-possessed innocence. This is exactly the role Clyde would like, and he assents to the fiction because it confirms his best image of himself and because Jephson offers him a model of strength and self-possession to emulate.

Jephson's defense, with another necessary irony, also confirms the court's legitimacy (which Dreiser himself questions at least a little) by constructing Clyde's case on the basis of his ability to make a free choice. Jephson maintains Clyde did intend to murder Roberta but responded to her pain and at the last moment changed his mind. As Dreiser has shown us, Clyde was not free enough to change his mind at that moment: paralyzed with fear and hysteria, he allowed her to drown.[4] Under the law, freedom is the freedom of intention, and this principle is ramified into meaning that intention also constitutes a legal "identity." But intention is not defi-

4. See Richard Lehan, *Theodore Dreiser: His World and His Novels* (Carbondale: Southern Illinois University Press, 1969), 168–69. Lehan argues that Clyde is legally innocent. Warren takes exception to Lehan's view in a long note in *Homage to Theodore Dreiser*, 159ff. Warren also develops some interesting arguments about McMillan's fate in an earlier version of the novel. This position does not quite square with Warren's earlier position on McMillan in an essay that was published as "*An American Tragedy*," *Yale Review*, LII (October, 1962), 1–15. This essay has been reprinted as the Introduction to the Meridian edition of the novel. Like Warren, I believe Clyde is legally guilty; but unlike him, I think Jephson is the novel's hero.

nitive. In instructing the jury, the judge says that the motive itself "may be shown as a *circumstance* to aid in *fixing* a crime, yet the people are not required to prove a motive." The meaning of the act, therefore, is legally more important than the full identity of the agent; the crime is more important to the court than the criminal is. Nonetheless, Clyde's counsel wants to exploit the ambiguous relationships between identity, motive, and circumstance by demonstrating conflicting motives and by extending the compass of relevant circumstance to include Clyde's whole life. In his opening presentation, Belknap argues that motive is not always unified and clear, as conventional institutions would have it. "I know that as you gentlemen view such things, such conduct has no excuse for being. One may be the victim of an internal conflict between two illicit moods, yet, nevertheless, as the law and church see it, guilty of sin and crime. But the truth, none-the-less, is that they do exist in the human heart, law or no law, religion or no religion, and in scores of cases they motivate the actions of the victims. And we admit they motivated the actions of Clyde Griffiths." Later in examining Clyde on the stand, Jephson develops this anti-institutional argument into the essence of the apology in Clyde's confession by trying to identify Clyde as a victim himself. " 'And it was because you were a moral and mental coward as I see it, Clyde—not that I am condemning you for anything you cannot help. (After all, you did not make yourself, did you?)' But this was too much, and the judge here cautioned him to use more discretion in framing his future questions."[5]

Clyde, however, does not understand the rationale of the apology Jephson is fashioning. Because he does not understand himself and is a coward, he does not see the value of candor; and because he has no articulate individuality at this point, he still defines himself in terms of the conventional assumptions he locates in "all the people throughout the entire United States." Clyde is an exception who proves the rule, because he is exactly Stephen Spender's generic outcast who "pleads with humanity to relate his isolation to its wholeness," rather than a character like Moll who can define a

5. Dreiser, *An American Tragedy*, 791, 723, 728.

smaller community. Speaking of Roberta with Jephson outside the court, Clyde says:

> "I don't know about the moral or mental courage," replied Clyde, a little hurt and irritated by this description of himself, "but I felt sorry for her just the same. She used to cry and I didn't have the heart to tell her anything."
>
> "I see. Well, let it stand that way if you want to. But now answer me one other thing. That relationship between you two—what about that—after you knew that you didn't care for her anymore. Did that continue?"
>
> "Well, no, sir, not so very long, anyhow," replied Clyde, most nervously and shamefacedly. He was thinking of all the people before him now—of his mother—Sondra—of all the people throughout the entire United States—who would read and so know. And on first being shown these questions weeks and weeks before he had wanted to know of Jephson what the use of all that was. And Jephson had replied: "Educational effect. The quicker and harder we can shock 'em with some of the real facts of life around here, the easier it is going to be for you to get a little more sane consideration of what your problem was. But don't worry your head over that now. When the time comes, just answer 'em and leave the rest to us. We know what we're doing."[6]

Jephson does know what he is doing, not only as Clyde's lawyer, but as his confessor too. When Clyde takes the stand, Jephson stands between him and the jury, so that Clyde can make his confession as though to Jephson alone. Moreover, in mediating for Clyde, Jephson also cross-examines him, asking the hard questions, attacking the weaknesses in Clyde's story, trying to absorb and neutralize the jury's skepticism and hostility. This tactic exposes more of the truth than Clyde desires, but it dramatizes Jephson's role as the representative of the kind of community in which Clyde could possess his full identity. Jephson is not at all like

6. *Ibid.*, 736.

Clyde; he is a strong, independent, successful man, with a "hard, *integrated* earnestness," yet he understands and accepts Clyde.[7] Still, the most devastating issue of Clyde's weakness is what it implies about the possibilities of personal relationships in Dreiser's world, and what this in turn implies about the efficacy of confession. For despite his efforts, Jephson can do nothing for Clyde personally. Since Clyde accepts himself as a criminal, he can accept Jephson only as his lawyer. Their relationship is functional, mechanized.

Not all personal relationships in *An American Tragedy* are so, however, and even Clyde knows that he needs the kind of personal confirmation that he believes would have come to him through Sondra's love. He loves Sondra because she is beautiful, wealthy, and superior, and more interesting, because she is "different from any one I had ever known—more independent—and everybody paid so much attention to what she did and what she said. She seemed to know more than any one else I ever knew." Clyde also thinks of her as "daring, too—not so simple or trusting as Miss Alden was—and at first it was hard for me to believe that she was becoming so interested in me."[8] Sondra is "daring" because her interest in Clyde defies Gilbert Griffiths and the hierarchy of Lycurgus (a city named for a Spartan tyrant of the ninth century B.C., whom Rousseau, by the way, admired greatly). What Clyde does not recognize is how much Sondra is like Jephson. What makes Jephson so important is that Sondra is prevented from providing Clyde with any help during his trial or making any kind of apology for him, because her family and the district attorney agree that she will not appear in court. In effect, they even take her identity from her; she is referred to only as "Miss X" and writes Clyde a letter that she cannot sign.

Yet, because Clyde cannot understand that Jephson offers him a similar, if more difficult, confirmation in the confession he has Clyde make, the confession fails. Clyde does not understand or

7. *Ibid.*, 649 (author's emphasis).
8. *Ibid.*, 739.

trust himself; he will not admit to his weaknesses, one of which is his fear of abandoning the role he is trying to play. So there is nothing he can say to the jury that is as affecting as the letters from Roberta that Mason reads aloud. The only juror with any reservations at all is Samuel Upham, who does not realize how much like Clyde he is. Upham holds out for a while, not because he has heard Clyde's confession and identifies with him, but because he too is "taken with the personality of Jephson."[9] Very quickly, however, Upham genuflects to social pressures and moves back into the local community that embraces Roberta as one of their own, condemns Clyde, and will continue to patronize Upham's drugstore. The upper classes of Lycurgus look down on Clyde; the lower classes of Bridgeburg hold him up for condemnation. No one can see Clyde as "one of us."

Dreiser never hedges the questions of Clyde's legal guilt; he never fails to point out, again and again, the lies Clyde tells. But Dreiser's fundamental concern is with Clyde's identity, and the end of the trial is not the end of Clyde's story. In jail, as he ponders his responsibility, Clyde begins to realize that his problem is too complex to be settled simply by the court's verdict and its definition of him. He seeks the help of the Reverend Duncan McMillan, who seems to be the perfect confessor. McMillan has Jephson's strength and the faith of Clyde's mother; and he encourages in Clyde the kind of personal relationship that issues from the intimacy and trust that make confession possible. And Clyde, after all his deceit and self-deception, is ready to discover himself, as he sees there is more to him "than he had been able yet to make clear, even to himself."[10]

Clyde's similarities to Moll Flanders at this point should be apparent. Both are guilty of capital crimes and face death. Moll in Newgate has her governess and the sympathetic clergyman, Clyde has his mother and McMillan. Here, unfortunately, the parallels

9. *Ibid.*, 792.

10. The "standard" view of McMillan is represented in F. O. Matthiessen, *Theodore Dreiser* (William Sloane Associates, 1951), 206–207. Dreiser, *An American Tragedy*, 851.

end. Clyde's confession is never fully realized, and even in his own mind his conversion is uncertain. But in this case the fault is not all Clyde's, because McMillan fails him. Dreiser says McMillan is passionate, independent, and nonsectarian, but he is also "confused."[11] McMillan cannot quite admit to his own confusion, cannot quite see himself in Clyde, and like the jury, cannot get beyond the single question of Clyde's guilt. He is finally less interested in the full truth of Clyde's bewilderment and weakness than he is in eliciting a more conservative statement about Clyde's culpability, which would confirm McMillan's pastoral role. He uses Clyde, who is left alone with his suffering, still unsure of who he is.

> In vain it was that McMillan now pointed out to Clyde that his awakened moral and spiritual understanding more perfectly and beautifully fitted him for life and action than ever before. He was alone. He had no one who believed in him. No one. He had no one, whom, in any of his troubled and tortured actions before that crime saw anything but the darkest guilt apparently. And yet—and yet—(and this despite Sondra and the Reverend McMillan and all the world for that matter, Mason, the jury at Bridgeburg, the court of Appeals at Albany, if it should decide to confirm the jury at Bridgeburg), he had a feeling in his heart that he was not as guilty as they all seemed to think.
>
> . . . .
>
> How sad. How hopeless. Would no one ever understand —or give him credit for his human—if all too human and perhaps wrong hungers—yet from which so many others—along with himself suffered?[12]

These "all too human and perhaps wrong hungers" are as close as Clyde can come to formulating his real identity. As he realizes he shares these hungers with "so many others," he also begins to formulate his sense of the kind of community he needs to recog-

11. Dreiser, *An American Tragedy*, 835.
12. *Ibid.*, 857, 864.

nize him. It is not the upper social class of Lycurgus, nor is it the orthodox community of believers that his mother and McMillan represent. It is the kind of community a fully realized confession could sponsor.

However, the confessional statement that McMillan supervises, after he has failed to win commutation from the new governor, contains no real indication of Clyde's growing self-consciousness. It is, rather, all impersonal formula, filled with McMillan's own words (as Dreiser points out in the parenthesis), and it is a fiction so pious that it amounts to a lie.

> In the shadow of the Valley of Death it is my desire to do everything that would remove any doubt as to my having found Jesus Christ, the personal Savior and unfailing friend. My one regret at this time is that I have not given Him the preeminence in my life while I had the opportunity to work for Him.
>
> If I could only say some one thing that would draw young men to Him I would deem it the greatest privilege ever granted me. But all I can say now is, "I know in whom I have believed, and am persuaded that He is able to keep that which I have committed unto Him against that day" (a quotation that McMillan had familiarized him with).
>
> If the young men of this country could only know the joy and pleasure of a Christian life, I know they would do all in their power to become earnest, active Christians, and would strive to have them live as Christ would have them live.
>
> There is not one thing I have left undone which will bar me from facing my God, knowing that my sins are forgiven, for I have been free and frank in my talks with my spiritual adviser and God knows where I stand.
>
> My task is done, the victory won.
>
> CLYDE GRIFFITHS[13]

The plug for McMillan is really damning. This letter would be, in

13. *Ibid.*, 867–68.

its own way, as outrageous as the Underground Man's letter to Simonov, if it were not for the obvious fact that Clyde does not believe it.

Perhaps the most terrible irony of *An American Tragedy* is that the court which condemns Clyde to death also acknowledges his freedom; and under Jephson's interpretation of motive and circumstance, the court is a much more open forum for the examination of the divisions and ambiguities that constitute Clyde's identity. McMillan's personal theology, on the other hand, is as rigid as the prejudices of the jurors. His emotion may make him a more attractive confessor than Jephson is, but Clyde comes closest to the truth in the confession he makes under Jephson's auspices. It is not necessary to argue whether Dreiser subscribes to democracy more than he does to religion. Both of Clyde's confessions fail because, as Dreiser clearly shows, nothing in Clyde's world can successfully foster the kind of community in which the individual's full identity can be recognized. Some individuals are weak, some are strong, but there are no personal relationships in the novel that are alleviating or redemptive.

Such a vision of modern life may not be exclusively Dreiser's, but what gives this tragedy its power and importance is that Dreiser has embodied in it his sense of the limitations of his own art. Neither Conrad nor Faulkner is notably optimistic, but in *Lord Jim* and *Absalom, Absalom!* they both use the confession to win some kind of accommodation for Jim, Marlow, Sutpen, maybe Rosa, and Quentin, for they both affirm the power of the sympathetic imagination and the possibilities of "fictions." *An American Tragedy* affirms nothing but Clyde's inability to possess himself; and his confessions fail because he can do nothing for himself, Sondra and Jephson can do nothing for him, and not even Dreiser can change the conditions of this world by his art. Naturalism assumes the immutability of both character and value. The weak remain weak and the strong may survive because they are strong to begin with; but both are finally powerless to effect any changes in their essential condition. Dreiser's own reliance on newspaper accounts of crimes similar to Clyde's is itself a sign of the limits the naturalist must honor in fidelity to his aesthetic beliefs; Dreiser uses the newspapers because he cannot honestly see the ground of another kind of truth. Like Dostoevsky, he can create a deeper sympathy for the criminal and present the murderer as his own victim as well; but unlike Dostoevsky, he cannot transform the facts to re-create their value. Neither can Jephson, who is Dreiser's portrait of the artist and as close to an heroic character as the novel has. Jephson's own fiction does as much with the facts of Clyde's life as possible. Jephson himself is skeptical, compassionate, and tough; his political acumen is an uncommon advantage; and his strength of character gives him a powerful presence. But he is helpless to do anything for Clyde personally.

The implication of Dreiser's art is that whatever the forces of human destiny may be called, they are forces impervious to alteration. Confession, on the other hand, assumes a world in which some changes, at least, are possible. Along these lines, Goethe has some stirring remarks.

> I must confess that I have always been suspicious of that great and so fine-sounding task, "Know thyself," as something of a stratagem of a secret conspiracy of priests who wanted to confuse men by making unrealisable demands of them, and to seduce them from activity directed towards the outside world to an inward and false contemplativeness. Man knows himself only in so far as he knows the world, and becomes aware of the world only in himself, and of himself only in it. Every new object, well observed, opens a new organ in us.[14]

No one has ever confused Dreiser with Goethe, who gave equal weight in his autobiography to both *Dichtung und Wahrheit*, and whose world was open and reciprocal, nutritive to the human imagination that fed it back. Dreiser's world is not. Reciprocation turns upon itself in a vicious empty circle. Even Dreiser's intense, sophisticated interest in modern science gave him no models for

14. Quoted in Roy Pascal, *Design and Truth in Autobiography* (Cambridge, Mass.: Harvard University Press, 1960), 46–47.

the kind of growth and self-realization implicitly possible in Goethe's guarded testament.[15] How could Clyde possibly know himself in a world that will not acknowledge him? Through people, with the honorable exception of Jephson, who will not admit the community of their own weakness and guilt?

I do not think it diminishes the greatness of Dreiser's novel to say that it opens no new organs in us in the way that *Notes from Underground* opens a new eye on the self.[16] For all his honesty, compassion, and patience, Dreiser makes a dark and oppressively intractable world, in which the solitary confinement of each of us is inescapable, even when we do try to confess to the crime of being ourselves. Dreiser's integrity can be as fierce as Sartre's ideology in showing us that there are no exits.

Gatsby confesses to Nick the night after Myrtle Wilson is killed, as he awaits the call from Daisy that never comes. He confesses because he has no more reason to hide his identity behind the elaborate masks that have inspired the people at his parties to pay him "the subtle tribute of knowing nothing whatever about him." Gatsby has always fostered the mysteries around him, and Nick's explanation of the sudden change is that " 'Jay Gatsby' had broken up like glass against Tom's hard malice, and the long secret extravaganza was played out. I think that he would have acknowledged anything now, without reserve, but he wanted to talk about Daisy."[17] He wants to talk about Daisy because she is the final cause of the extravaganza and the justification of Gatsby's long performance. Though Nick is sympathetic to Gatsby's readiness to open up, he does not quite understand the reason. For Gatsby has really broken against Daisy's failure to fulfill his conception of her, to realize his dream, and to confirm him in his brave imposture. After the accident, she is reconciled with Tom, whose

15. For a discussion of Dreiser's scientific interests, see Ellen Moers, *The Two Dreisers* (New York: Viking Press, 1969), Pt. 4, Chaps. 3 and 4.

16. Lionel Trilling, *Beyond Culture* (New York: Viking Press, 1968), 57–87.

17. F. Scott Fitzgerald, *The Great Gatsby* (New York: Charles Scribner's Sons, 1953), 61, 148.

selfishness is more brutal but less demanding than Gatsby's. So in explaining his life with Dan Cody and the fatal surprise of falling in love with Daisy, Gatsby tries to explain who he is and how he came to be. This confession signals the clear end of one phase of his life, which began the moment on Lake Superior when he boarded Cody's yacht and announced himself to be Jay Gatsby, and it helps him to begin another phase.

The manner of any confession is always determined by the matters to be confessed and by the character of the confessor. According to this principle, we do not hear much of Gatsby's confession directly because Nick, unlike Jephson, is always free to mediate and interpret, and this is not the first time Gatsby has confided in him. He has trusted Nick to arrange the meeting with Daisy, insisted that he stay around while he shows Daisy the house, and demanded that Nick remain in the Plaza suite while he has it out with Tom. Moreover, Gatsby is not confessing to a crime; he is confessing his identity, and he has a much clearer idea than Clyde of who he is and why he has done what he has. Perhaps the most important aspect of his revelations, however, is Gatsby's unself-consciousness. He expresses the most extraordinary ideas about himself without even realizing that these ideas need an explanation or defense. "Can't repeat the past? . . . Why of course you can!" he has said to Nick in talking about Daisy. And as he makes his confession, he dismisses Daisy's love for Tom with, "In any case . . . it was just personal." Nick's immediate response is an apology: "What could you make of that, except to suspect some intensity in his conception of the affair that couldn't be measured?"[18] This intensity of conception Gatsby expresses in gestures that are more fully articulated than his explanations, and Nick understands what is a fairly laconic confession because he has already witnessed Gatsby at his most expressive—yearning toward the green light; frozen in a solitary farewell at the end of a party; nervous and clumsy as he meets Daisy again; both radiant and inexplicably disappointed as he shows her the house and dis-

18. *Ibid.*, 111, 152.

penses his sacramental shirts. Most poignant and expressive of all are Gatsby's refusal to let Daisy take the blame for Myrtle's death, his refusal to abandon her, and his need to talk to Nick when she abandons him. Until this point, Gatsby has been making it so well on luck and intuition that he has seldom had to examine himself or his assumptions; the simple need to confess, however, to have the support of Nick's company, is an act by which he admits that his identity is no longer comprehended by a world he no longer masters.

In his longest statement to Nick, Gatsby sounds modest, even innocent, as he explains the start of his fall. "I can't describe to you how surprised I was to find out I loved her, old sport. I even hoped for a while that she'd throw me over, but she didn't, because she was in love with me too. She thought I knew a lot because I knew different things from her. . . . Well, there I was, 'way off my ambitions, getting deeper in love every minute, and all of a sudden I didn't care. What was the use of doing great things if I could have a better time telling her what I was going to do?"[19] This statement does a lot to rescue Gatsby from mere vulgarity and ambition, for in it he identifies himself as the James Gatz who became Jay Gatsby and eventually needed Daisy Fay's confirmation of that identity. This statement also shows how trusting and intimate the mysterious Gatsby has become, how ready he is now to disclose himself. On the other hand, the things Gatsby does not say in his confession are as important as the things he does. Obviously, there is no way he can declare to Nick, "You know, old sport, I *am* the Platonic conception of myself," because he does not have the cultural vocabulary, to say the least, nor does he have the extrapersonal sense of himself that even Clyde has in the eyes of "all the people throughout the entire United States." (In Jim and Sutpen, this extrapersonal sense of the self amounts to a vision of destiny.) Although Gatsby seems to apologize for getting " 'way off my ambitions, getting deeper in love every minute," he does not mention, much less apologize for, his criminal acti-

19. *Ibid.*, 150.

vities. This suggests that Gatsby's actions, however expressive and definitive of him, are much less important to him than his intentions. He does not see himself as others see him, which is both his strength and tragic flaw; he has imagined himself into being without understanding the significance of the image he projects. This fact makes his rare self-revelations all the more important, especially his confession to Nick, because Gatsby's unself-consciousness and innocence have blinded him and become self-destructive.[20] He cannot understand why Daisy cries over his beautiful shirts; he apparently cannot understand why she leaves him.

Somewhere behind every confession is a conversionary experience, a significant change that makes a clearer understanding of the self necessary. Gatsby's confession to Nick is so muted, however, and he dies so soon after making it, that it is hard to define exactly the meaning of the conversion that losing Daisy effects in his life. His confession is an act of self-renewal; it explains his past and exemplifies his "romantic readiness" for the future; but it is so unapologetic that it does not allow us to foresee a future for Gatsby in the way we can foresee a future for Moll, the Underground Man, and Ishmael.[21] Still, Gatsby seems to be in good shape, according to the rule of thumb I have proposed: the more sure of himself the speaker is, the less rhetorical or apologetic his confession will be; the better he knows himself and his confessor, the less he will have to say to justify himself. A corollary of this rule, however, is that the apology implicitly defines the meaning of the conversion. Perhaps Gatsby's lack of apology means he has not changed at all, that he makes his confession to Nick simply to clarify himself and maintain his "readiness." However, Nick

20. A very different view of Gatsby's character is offered by Marius Bewley, *The Eccentric Design* (New York: Columbia University Press, 1959), 276–77. See also Milton B. Stern, *The Golden Moment: The Novels of F. Scott Fitzgerald* (Urbana: University of Illinois Press, 1970), 166–67. Although I cannot disagree with their ideas about mythic character, I think Gatsby's confession gives him another aspect that must also be recognized.

21. Fitzgerald, *The Great Gatsby*, 2.

realizes that Gatsby's career and character do need some explanation; and just as Nick absorbs the apologetic function that Gatsby's confession demands, so too he enacts the conversionary experience that usually inspires the confession.

Nick's defense of Gatsby is built on his understanding that Gatsby is the Platonic conception of himself. Nick cannot bring Daisy back to revivify Gatsby's dream, but he does understand Gatsby in some ways better than Gatsby understands himself (as Jephson does Clyde, as Marlow does Jim), and he can provide a kind of confirmation for Gatsby that even Daisy cannot. As Nick leaves Gatsby, he turns and shouts: "They're a rotten crowd. . . . You're worth the whole damn bunch put together." This is a far cry from calling Gatsby great, but it signals an important change in Nick and seems sufficient for Gatsby, whose "face broke into that radiant and understanding smile, as if we'd been in ecstatic cahoots on that fact all the time."[22] These "ecstatic cahoots" are important, for they signify that Gatsby has created through Nick's audience the beginnings of a better quality of relationship. They signify as well the great difference between *An American Tragedy* and *The Great Gatsby.* No one of Dreiser's characters has the freedom or power to surpass socially determined roles in order to enter the more important moral unions in which identities can be freely realized and communities made. "Ecstatic cahoots," despite the absurdity of the phrase itself, is a sign of the conversion in Nick's ideas that makes Gatsby much more than the "elegant young roughneck" Nick once thought him to be and Nick himself more than Gatsby's accidental neighbor. Ultimately, therefore, Gatsby has his vindication because Nick makes Gatsby "great"; and through Gatsby, Nick slowly acquires the sense of a new identity that separates him from all the "careless" people he once thought he was part of.[23] In hearing Gatsby's confession, Nick himself discovers the chance to become good.

22. *Ibid.*, 154.

23. This is also the argument of Thomas A. Hanzo, "The Theme and the Narrator of *The Great Gatsby,*" *Modern Fiction Studies*, II (Winter, 1956–57),

From what Gatsby tells him, Nick constructs an apology more complicated and visionary than anything Jephson is allowed to make of Clyde's confession. Nick is free to paraphrase most of Gatsby's original words and to add ideas about Gatsby that make Gatsby's story a romance. Of the many ways in which to define romance and romantic characterization, the most succinct formulation for our purpose is provided by Scholes and Kellogg: "Where mimetic narrative aims at a psychological reproduction of mental process, romantic narrative presents thought in the form of rhetoric."[24] *The Great Gatsby's* mimesis is in the dramatization of Nick's mental process; its romance is in Nick's ideas about Gatsby, which are couched in the rhetoric Nick uses to drop Plato's name and to allude to Keats and Coleridge. Nick is also free from naturalistic chronology and from having to obey strictly the laws of cause and effect. He creates a spatial field for the disposition of the narrative, so that the whole story of Gatsby and his dream does not have to come simply in the wake of Gatsby's failure and death. More important, however, is that because Gatsby has made his confession at a moment when Nick says he "had reached the point of believing everything and nothing about him," Nick extrudes Gatsby's apology through his own skepticism, confusion, and resistance. This rhetorical strategy is something Jephson attempts in his cross-examination of Clyde, and Nick and Jephson both work to become the inimical "strange children" in a way that the Reverend McMillan never can. For both Jephson and Nick, though, skepticism is more than a calculated strategy; it is a natural response. In Nick's case, his skepticism keeps his account more honest and credible; it preserves some of Gatsby's necessary mystery and factitiousness; and it dramatizes the conversion Nick undergoes in the process of discovering himself. After Gatsby's death he finds himself on "Gatsby's side, and alone" and also finds that he too is an outsider, an insight that provides a focus for

183–90. Hanzo's reading represents the "orthodox" view of Nick's role and reliability.

24. Robert Scholes and Robert Kellogg, *The Nature of Narrative* (London: Oxford University Press, 1968), 14.

him and precipitates a crisis in him that reveals more clearly the needs he has never quite acknowledged to himself.[25]

Before he becomes Gatsby's confessor, Nick has been a man of some parts but hazy definition. From the provinces himself and restless after the European war, he too comes East to enter the bond business, which is for him less like a vocation than a fraternity. Nick's aristocratic reserve has already made him the confessor of many young men whom he has only condescended to listen to, yet he calls his rectitude a "matter of infinite hope." His apparent receptiveness, however, is a talent Nick values very little, seems to fear, and never uses deliberately. His ability to listen appears to be a sign of his own indeterminacy, the basis of his unacknowledged needs, and the source of his confusion. In the eyes of others, though, Nick holds his poise so well that they seek his ratification. As soon as she can, in Chapter 1, Daisy tells him of her difficulties and unhappiness. In Chapter 2, Tom seeks Nick's approval of Myrtle, who is eager herself to explain her relationship with Tom. Even Meyer Wolfsheim, a very cautious man, wants to confide in Nick his affiliation with Gatsby. Throughout the novel, there is a great need for intimacy on the part of almost everyone but Jordan Baker, with whom Nick eventually falls in love. As he says, "Almost any exhibition of complete self-sufficiency draws a stunned tribute from me."[26]

Nick's affair with Jordan is illuminating in many ways. He prides himself on honesty, and she is an habitual liar; he is "slow-thinking and full of interior rules," and she is fast, self-indulgent, and heedless. She is a handsome, toney companion around New York, but her most inspiring quality seems to be her knowledge of Gatsby's love for Daisy. What Jordan tells Nick about Louisville delivers Gatsby "from the womb of his purposeless splendor" and seems to give birth to Nick's love for Jordan.[27] Gatsby's purity and devotion, implicit in Jordan's apology for him, strike Nick as both surprising and encouraging, for they all occupy a world of

25. Fitzgerald, *The Great Gatsby*, 102, 165.
26. *Ibid.*, 1, 9.
27. *Ibid.*, 79.

missed "gonnegtions." There is not a single good marriage in the novel, and the parties Gatsby gives, which promise magic, end in tawdry violence.

Moreover, Nick naturally spends much of his time being lonely: he eats alone ("the gloomiest event of my day"), scouts women on Fifth Avenue but pursues them only in his mind, and tries to disguise his self-pity by projecting his loneliness onto other young men. This loneliness is steepest when, on the afternoon Tom and Gatsby fight in the Plaza, he realizes it is his thirtieth birthday: "Thirty—the promise of a decade of loneliness, a thinning list of single men to know, a thinning briefcase of enthusiasm, thinning hair. But there was Jordan beside me, who, unlike Daisy, was too wise ever to carry well-forgotten dreams from age to age. As we passed over the dark bridge her wan face fell lazily against my coat's shoulder and the formidable stroke of thirty died away with the reassuring pressure of her hand." Unaggressive and susceptible to the sentimentality of failure, Nick himself will later harbor "well-forgotten dreams." And though he always tries to be honest, he deludes himself here with an image of his own self-possession, as mirrored by Jordan's hard, slick surface. His loneliness and emotional need only augment the confusion that is most apparent in the pains it takes him to be "honest" with her when they finally part and she calls him a "bad driver."[28] Without knowing who he is at the moment, Nick does not know exactly what he is being honest about, and Jordan has neither the time nor inclination to hear whatever kind of confession Nick could make himself. (Fitzgerald says in his notebooks, "No such thing as a man willing to be honest—that would be like a blind man willing to see.")[29]

Nick, however, has less trouble with the honesty of his responses to Gatsby. Sickened by the accident, he leaves Jordan at the Buchanans' and prefers, characteristically, to be alone. Gatsby calls to him from the bushes and Nick attends.[30] Even more "self-

28. *Ibid.*, 57, 136, 179.

29. F. Scott Fitzgerald, *The Crack Up*, ed. Edmund Wilson (New York: New Directions, 1956), 124.

30. Fitzgerald, *The Great Gatsby*, 143–44.

sufficient" and grandly dishonest than Jordan, Gatsby is nonetheless more intimate and honestly vulnerable. And if Nick confirms him, it is because Gatsby has already done the same for Nick, the first time they meet.

> He smiled understandingly—much more than understandingly. It was one of those rare smiles with a quality of eternal reassurance in it, that you may come across four or five times in life. It faced—or seemed to face—the whole external world for an instant, and then concentrated on *you* with an irresistible prejudice in your favor. It understood you just as far as you wanted to be understood, believed in you as you would like to believe in yourself, and assured you that it had precisely the impression of you that, at your best, you hoped to convey.[31]

Gatsby is not usually plagued by sensitivity to other people; he uses them, even at his parties, and often tries to buy them off, as he subsequently tries to buy Nick off with a deal. And Gatsby is socially clumsy. When his smile fades, he seems to Nick stiff and absurd. (When he arranges Nick's meeting with Jordan, he begins with, "Look here, old sport . . . what's your opinion of me anyhow?")[32] What Nick sees in Gatsby's smile, therefore, is clearly something he wants to see: the smile assures him of his best self-image but does not exceed the boundaries of privacy. No confessor could offer a smile of more perfectly unquestioning confirmation. "Every new object, well observed, opens a new organ in us," and Nick's explanation of Gatsby's first smile is probably the most important single thing he says about *himself* in the novel: in every case, the second-person pronouns actually mean Nick himself. Gatsby repeats this smile as he leaves Nick for the last time, sanctioning their "ecstatic cahoots," and together these smiles constitute an image of community, a moment of grace from which Nick never wants to fall.

31. *Ibid.*, 48.
32. *Ibid.*, 65.

Nick's subsequent apology for Gatsby is his attempt to return those smiles, to explain the meaning of his own conversion even if he cannot fully explain the meaning of Gatsby's. As he writes out his manuscript two years after Gatsby's death, Nick is honest enough to expose his own behavior and to face Gatsby's meretriciousness, but he seems unwilling to face himself as fully as he does Gatsby. His conversion turns him from the East toward his original community and its apparently more sustaining order of values, but there is no record of what he undergoes in making this transition, of how he explains it to anyone at home. Like Gatsby, Nick mutes the apologetic elements of his own story; but unlike Gatsby, he does not have so clearly defined an audience. He does not have Jephson's jury or Marlow's ready listeners. Rather, his communication with his reader is similar to his father's communication with him, and he trusts his reader to understand him as he has understood his father. "Whenever you feel like criticizing any one," his father told him, "just remember that all the people in this world haven't had the advantages that you've had." Nick says: "He didn't say any more, but we've always been unusually communicative in a reserved way, and I understood that he meant a great deal more than that." Trusting his reader as his father has trusted him explains some of Nick's reserve; and he may be defining the kind of audience he needs in a most flattering and intimate way, by trusting them to understand of him "a great deal more than that." On the other hand, such filial piety in a man of Nick's age and experience is surprising, especially since Nick has had a "feeling of defiance, of scornful solidarity between Gatsby and me against them all."[33] His solidarity with Gatsby he explains very well, but his defiance and scorn are somewhat dissipated in his final account, and this leads us to consider two important formal qualities of his narrative that exemplify its attitude toward itself and toward literature.

Many confessions, as they define the antagonistic audience, also attack the conventions of literature, the system of expectations

33. *Ibid.*, 1, 166.

that would prevent the conventional reader from hearing the truth of the confession. Both Moll and her editor worry about the reader who would want her story to be one of crime and punishment only. The Underground Man is brilliant and ruthless at manipulating his literary audience of gentlemen. Felix Krull is always attacking art in the name of truth, even as he tries to explain art's power and freedom. And Ishmael undercuts his own book in order to persuade us to go whaling ourselves. Moreover, in many novels of the young man from the provinces, there is a "generic" preoccupation with the relationship between the elements of a novel of manners and the elements of a romance. In such novels, manners are explained, exposed, and corrected in the kind of satire that goes into creating Nick's list of the names of the people who attend Gatsby's parties; and romance is measured in terms of transcendence, the degree to which the young man achieves superiority to the values and historical determination of his original environment.[34] *Red and Black*, for instance, contains a great deal of romance, whereas *An American Tragedy* contains none. In Dickens' *Great Expectations* and in *Crime and Punishment*, the amount of transcendence one attributes to Pip and Raskolnikov accurately reflects one's sense of each book's moral arguments about freedom and responsibility.

Nick seems fully aware of the tension between manners and romance in Gatsby's case; indeed, his whole argument is that Gatsby is not merely the man who gave those fabulous parties. But Nick's taste for satire, the scorn and defiance he once felt, do not move him to attack literary conventions. Consequently, though he does argue his case for Gatsby through his skepticism and confusion, he never explicitly defines his own antagonist—the kind of reader who would simply laugh at Gatsby's smile. He does define an unthreatening audience that is much less open and reciprocal than the kind of audience he figures in his father. These are people "in uniform and at a sort of moral attention forever," people who

34. For the best description of the novels of the young man from the provinces, see Lionel Trilling, *The Liberal Imagination* (Garden City, N.Y.: Doubleday, 1953), 58–61.

want "no more riotous excursions with privileged glimpses into the human heart." Nick has transcended himself somewhat by writing about his own "privileged glimpses" into Gatsby's heart, but he does not turn the "riotous excursion" of his experience into his own confession. The ultimate reach of his apology is to justify Gatsby by making him mythic, to elevate him into the realm of the Dutch sailors who disembarked onto the "fresh, green breast of the new world"—the last thing commensurate in historical experience to man's "capacity to wonder." In confessing to Nick, Gatsby has explained his fall by talking about falling in love with Daisy and wanting to talk to her. Nick later translates Gatsby's moment of transformation into the mythic terms of the kiss on the sidewalk by which Gatsby "forever wed his unutterable visions to her perishable breath."[35]

Although it is easy to take advantage of Nick's rhetoric, his literary imagination complements, even dignifies, Gatsby's intuitive powers of self-conception; his mythic apology redeems Gatsby's naïvete and makes much more of him than the good-bad guy that American movies have made a favorite icon. To take such a character and make him so explicitly mythic proves Fitzgerald's own intuition and courage. Nonetheless, Nick's literary maneuvers with Gatsby's confession do violate to some extent Gatsby's own courage and example, and they impede Nick's complete self-realization. Confessions find their end in community, but confession is an open-ended form and faces the future. Because Nick does not make his own confession, because he does elevate Gatsby to a mythic altitude, he tries to close off his own story and experience. Commenting on the famous last lines of the novel—"Gatsby believed in the green light, the orgiastic future that year by year recedes before us. It eluded us then, but that's no matter—tomorrow we will run faster, stretch out our arms farther. . . . And one fine morning—So we beat on, boats against the current, borne back ceaselessly into the past."—Alan Friedman says: "The narrator Nick Carraway's final sentence reflects his (and Fitzgerald's)

35. Fitzgerald, *The Great Gatsby*, 2, 182, 150, 112.

need to put a containing limit on his experience, here ironic of course: since the experience of Gatsby (both the experience *by* Gatsby himself and the experience of Gatsby *by* the narrator) will really allow no such limit. The two motions, Gatsby's vainly into the future, Carraway's vainly into the past, are held together in the last sentence; the opposed currents of conscience locked there in an unrelieved tension."[36] Gatsby's motion into the future is not so vain as Friedman suggests, because his confession is realized in Nick's conversion and narrative; but Nick's attempt to limit Gatsby and his own experience of Gatsby is, I think, as vain as Friedman makes it. Because Nick seems not to understand all the implications of making Gatsby mythic, he opens himself to questions about his own credibility.

Nick is not so unreliable or self-deceiving as Robert Stallman indicates, and he can be defended on the grounds that his act of writing is an honest and successful attempt at self-realization.[37] Yet the most interesting argument against Nick is made by Gary J. Scrimgeour, who contrasts *The Great Gatsby* and *Heart of Darkness*, and Nick and Marlow. Scrimgeour demonstrates quite persuasively the rhetorical advantage Marlow has in addressing his story to a live audience. Scrimgeour does not say that Marlow is making a confession, but Marlow *is* making a confession to his old friends aboard the *Nellie*, as he tries to explain his attachment to Kurtz and to justify the lies he has told on Kurtz's behalf. Although most of his old friends fail him and become his antagonists by falling asleep, the frame narrator remains awake to become Marlow's confessor and apologist, and a positive model for the reader. Because of this rhetorical structure, Scrimgeour maintains,

36. Alan Friedman, *The Turn of the Novel* (London: Oxford University Press, 1966), 33.

37. See R. W. Stallman, *The Houses that James Built and Other Literary Studies* (East Lansing: Michigan State University Press, 1961), 131–50. The best defense of Nick as a writer is made by Charles Thomas Samuels, "The Greatness of 'Gatsby,'" *Massachusetts Review*, VII (Autumn, 1966), 183–94. See also David L. Minter, *The Interpreted Design* (New Haven, Conn.: Yale University Press, 1969). His eighth chapter is a powerful defense of Nick as writer and seer.

Heart of Darkness is a more hopeful book than *Gatsby*, for Conrad has committed Marlow to continue his search whereas Fitzgerald has permitted Nick the complacency of closure.[38]

It is unfair to criticize *The Great Gatsby* for not doing something the reader would want—in this case, contain Nick's confession—especially when it is so successful at using the mode of romance to criticize and transcend manners. Nonetheless, because a confession is at its center and because Nick does acknowledge the need for community in returning home, *The Great Gatsby* stops short of realizing the full formal extension it would have if Nick were to identify more clearly his own confessor and admit, by doing this, that he alone cannot resolve the meaning of the Great Gatsby. What encourages me to offer this argument is that *The Great Gatsby* does contain the figure of a possible audience who stands beween Nick's father and the people Nick wants at moral attention. This figure is the "owl-eyed" man, who has understood long before Nick that Gatsby is a "regular Belasco" and who knows at Gatsby's funeral that Gatsby is also a "poor son-of-a-bitch." This, too, is a far cry from calling Gatsby great, but it does suggest that Fitzgerald sees a middle range of response to Gatsby that escapes the extremes of his guests' indifference and Nick's high nostalgia. The owl-eyed man could have become a figure like the skeptical French lieutenant Marlow must confront in *Lord Jim* or the "privileged man" Marlow chooses to test his final conclusions against. The development of such a figure would give Nick's argument more rigor than it has, and it would extend Nick into the kind of community he seeks, but takes too much for granted, in simply going home. Without such an audience to confront, Nick remains as personally alone as he has always been,

38. Gary J. Scrimgeour, "Against *The Great Gatsby*," *Criticism*, VIII (Winter, 1966), 75–86. A good counterargument to Scrimgeour's is Jerome Thale's in "The Narrator as Hero," *Twentieth Century Literature*, III (July, 1957), 69–73. The most thorough and suggestive study of Conrad and Fitzgerald is Robert E. Long, "*The Great Gatsby* and the Tradition of Joseph Conrad," *Texas Studies in Language and Literature*, VIII (Summer–Fall, 1966), 257–76 and 407–22.

committed to a dead man and locked into a sentimentality that he wants to pass off as the ineffable.[39]

At a crucial moment in the narrative, Nick says: "Through all he said, even through his appalling sentimentality, I was reminded of something—an elusive rhythm, a fragment of lost words, that I had heard somewhere a long time ago. For a moment a phrase tried to take shape in my mouth and my lips parted like a dumb man's, as though there was more struggling upon them than a wisp of startled air. But they made no sound, and what I had almost remembered was uncommunicable forever." This paragraph follows immediately Nick's description of the kiss by which Gatsby "wed his unutterable visions" to Daisy's "perishable breath." Yet, Gatsby's visions cannot be that unutterable, for Nick himself has given them convincing utterance and a mythic interpretation, and the only evidence we have of Gatsby's "appalling sentimentality" is couched in Nick's own rhetoric. In another mood, he can say of Gatsby: "He took what he could get, ravenously and unscrupulously—eventually he took Daisy one still October night, took her because he had no real right to touch her hand."[40] This suggests that Nick can be clear-headed, even a bit cynical, about the connections between ambition and sex. So, his penchant for the ineffable is, like his description of Gatsby's smile, more revelatory of Nick himself than of Gatsby. Next to the skepticism of Marlow or Mr. Compson, for instance, Nick's words are merely a fashionable gesture towards the limitations of language that Nick himself undercuts with the powerful rhetoric of the novel's final pages.[41] With such rhetoric Nick indicates not only that he does want to close off Gatsby and his experience of Gatsby, but also that he aspires to the kind of "complete self-sufficiency" that impressed him in Jordan Baker and even more in Gatsby. Nick makes no confession himself because he does not fully understand the point of Gatsby's confession, and he wants to defend Gatsby by

39. See Bewley, *Eccentric Design*, 270–71, for a very different reaction to this passage.

40 Fitzgerald, *The Great Gatsby*, 112, 149.

41 See Stern, *Golden Moment*, 176, for a similar opinion.

a self-sufficient act of the independent imagination, which is the quality in Gatsby he admires the most. Nick seems to forget, finally, the importance of "ecstatic cahoots."

Nick is not the only one of Fitzgerald's characters who has trouble making a good confession and prefers the independence of the imagination. In "Absolution," which Fitzgerald at one time foresaw as a kind of prelude to *Gatsby*, eleven-year-old Rudolph Miller lies in the confessional itself by saying that he never lies.[42] (Nick says at one point, "I am one of the few honest people that I have ever known.")[43] When Rudolph tries to repair his sin by going to the parish rectory, he faces the crazy Father Schwartz, who is totally incapable of escaping his own neurotic fantasy life to hear what Rudolph is trying to tell him. Rudolph resolves the problem for himself by escaping into his imaginary alter ego, Blatchford Sarnemington. This transformation-escape anticipates, in a way, the moment James Gatz tells Dan Cody he is Jay Gatsby, and this kind of transformation, this preference for an imaginative identity to a real one, runs throughout Fitzgerald's work in the stories of the young men who want to be someone or something else. Rudolph also prefigures Nick, who prefers the mythic Gatsby to the confessional one and who would rather conceive of himself as myth maker than confessor. But one crucial difference between Rudolph and the other two is their ages.

Fitzgerald's difficulties with the confessional impulse are also to be seen in the autobiographical essays that are now the center of *The Crack Up*. These three essays deal with the painful experience of Fitzgerald's dissolution and putative failure; but what is most revealing about them is Fitzgerald's utter lack of interest or trust in his audience. Alfred Kazin has called *The Crack Up* "an American confession."[44] It was put together after Fitzgerald's death by Edmund Wilson, whom Fitzgerald identified as a kind of confessor

42 For another discussion of "Absolution," see Henry Dan Piper, *F. Scott Fitzgerald: A Critical Portrait* (New York: Holt, Rinehart and Winston, 1965), 104–107.

43. Fitzgerald, *The Great Gatsby*, 60.

44. Alfred Kazin, "An American Confession," in Alfred Kazin (ed.),

in his references to Wilson as his literary conscience, but Wilson was not the intended audience, as Kazin points out. Fitzgerald wrote the three essays for the readership of *Esquire* magazine, whom he mistakenly expected to satisfy quite easily. Fitzgerald himself admits to this mistake at the beginning of the second essay, "Handle with Care," when he apologizes for the inadequacies of the first piece, "The Crack-Up": "Your editor thought the article suggested too many aspects without regarding them closely, and probably many readers felt the same way—and there are always those to whom all self-revelation is contemptible, unless it ends with a noble thanks to the gods for the Unconquerable Soul." "Your editor"—not "mine"—is obviously not the man Nick Carraway's father was; and the crack about the "Unconquerable Soul" is more desperate than anything we hear from Gatsby. In the midst of this same essay, Fitzgerald takes another slap at the reader by saying: "(I have the sense of lecturing now, looking at a watch on the desk before me and seeing how many more minutes—)." This kind of condescension becomes a "witty" self-abasement, worthy of the Underground Man, when Fitzgerald closes the last piece of the trilogy, "Pasting it Together," with: "I will try to be a correct animal though, and if you throw me a bone with enough meat on it I may even lick your hand." These are terribly saddening words; the reader deserves more respect for the sympathetic powers of his own imagination, and Fitzgerald deserves a better self-regard. But he has virtually predicted the failure of these essays on failure when he says, at the beginning of the first piece, that only in "moments of weakness" do we "tell our friends" about the blows in life that have rendered it all a "process of breaking down."[45]

F. Scott Fitzgerald: The Man and his Work (Cleveland: World, 1951), 172. Many essays in this volume discuss *The Crack Up*, and one of its most enthusiastic supporters is Mark Schorer, "Fitzgerald's Tragic Sense," 169–71. See also Robert Sklar, *F. Scott Fitzgerald: The Last Laocoon* (New York: Oxford University Press, 1967), 309–11. Sklar argues that these essays are Fitzgerald's confessional act of self-renewal. He has also argued that Nick too is ready to renew himself as he begins to write—see 175.

45. F. Scott Fitzgerald, *The Crack Up*, ed. Edmund Wilson (New York: New Directions, 1956), 4, 10, 15, 22.

Dreiser wrote several autobiographical volumes, which John Berryman has said are "very like his novels and not much less interesting."[46] Although *A Book About Myself* is in no way a formal confession, it does not fail to record the pain in Dreiser's life at a time when he was about Clyde's age.

> Well, then, I was a coward. Could I stand up and defend myself against a man of my own height and weight? I doubted it, particularly if he were well-trained. In consequence I was again a coward. There was no hope for me among decently courageous men. Could I play tennis, baseball, football? No, not successfully. Assuredly I was a weakling of the worst kind. Nearly everybody could do those things, and nearly all youths were far more proficient in all the niceties of life than I: manners, dancing, knowledge of dress and occasions. Hence I was a fool. The dullest athlete of the least proficiency could overcome me: the most minute society man, if socially correct, was infinitely my superior. Hence what had I to hope for? And when it came to wealth and opportunity, how poor I seemed! No girl of real beauty and force would have anything to do with a man who was not a success; and so there I was, a complete failure to begin with.[47]

This may not be a distinguished passage, but it is not glib, and Dreiser does not condescend to the reader as Fitzgerald does in *The Crack Up.* Although Dreiser could not finally believe in the transforming power a confession can have for both its speaker and audience, he did understand the longing behind the confessional impulse with more insight and compassion than Fitzgerald, perhaps for the simple reason that he better understood failure.

It is not my purpose to conclude that *An American Tragedy* is a better novel than *The Great Gatsby,* according to a confes-

46. John Berryman, "Dreiser's Imagination," in Alfred Kazin and Charles Shapiro (eds.), *The Stature of Theodore Dreiser* (Bloomington: Indiana University Press, 1955), 149.

47. Theodore Dreiser, *A Book About Myself* (New York: Boni and Liveright, 1922), 107–108.

sional standard. They are novels that demonstrate how confession can be used within other forms, and both show how difficult making a confession can be, how important the right confessor is, and how wise Goethe was in insisting that self-knowledge is dependent upon a knowledge of the world. Listening to the confessions of Moll, the Underground Man, and Ishmael, we can be deceived about the confessional act's ease of realization, for they confront their confessors in prose rather than in person. Listening to Clyde as he confronts Jephson, the jury, and McMillan is another matter; so, too, is watching Gatsby's ease and Nick's reluctance in finding their audiences. In judging any confession's value or success, we must keep in mind the confessional act's natural provenance—its source in personal crisis and its uncertainties, embarrassments, and pain, even before the most sympathetic of confessors. If the confessional form illuminates from within the structures and formal attitudes of *An American Tragedy* and *The Great Gatsby*, Dreiser's naturalism and Fitzgerald's romanticism show us some of the impediments, both temperamental and aesthetic, that the confession must face and comprehend.

Furthermore, from the different ways in which they use the confession, we can deduce some conclusions about Dreiser and Fitzgerald, if the draw is gentle. Dreiser's careful handling of both of Clyde's attempts at a confession proves that he is not the simple, clumsy giant of compassion and the factual surface that is so often his caricature. He is not a great prose stylist, but he does have the sense of form necessary to any artist of consequence. Fitzgerald, on the other hand, is a great stylist, whose precocity sometimes seems to have blinded him to the deeper problems of form. Think of his indecision about the order of *Tender is the Night* and the growing maturity that his redactions of it manifest. The first version has a much more brilliant, stylish opening, but the second version, issued posthumously by Malcolm Cowley, has a much more powerful and honest narrative.

Yet perhaps the most interesting thing about Dreiser and Fitzgerald is that they share a tragic vision of society. Their methods of observation are very different: Dreiser's vision is more political, and his style works by documentary accretion; Fitzgerald's is more social, and his style works by brilliant epitomes. But, for both of them, the individual has very little chance to realize his identity in a sustaining community. Clyde and Gatsby both find adequate confessors; but Jephson is thwarted by political circumstances for which Dreiser cannot find an honest aesthetic solution; and Nick is thwarted finally by his own character, which resorts to aesthetics too readily. Nick, especially, denies the comic possibilities of confession by emphasizing the romantic nature of character, both Gatsby's and his own. Romantic characters, as Northrop Frye says, are characters "*in vacuo* idealized by revery."[48] This formula fits the youthful Gatsby and also comes to fit Nick as he idealizes Gatsby instead of bringing him into a living community.

Dreiser's insistence that Clyde is "one of us" is recognized by Jephson and by Dreiser's reader. Fitzgerald, on the other hand, seems to want to make Gatsby better than we are; and Nick wants to be one with Gatsby. This is not a mark of *The Great Gatsby*'s failure, but a sign of its romantic ambitions toward tragedy. However, the formal possibilities of *The Great Gatsby* do not make it so inevitably tragic as the formal assumptions of *An American Tragedy* make it. Clyde and Gatsby both die. Jephson's future becomes irrelevant when the higher court dismisses his appeal. Nick's future, however, is completely open when he leaves the East. But he closes it off by consigning Gatsby to myth and eliminating the possibilities inherent in Gatsby's confession. Conrad's Marlow is not unaware that Lord Jim has mythic properties, but he does better by Jim than Nick does by Gatsby because he carries Jim's story back into the community Jim knew he needed. Nick's characterization, insofar as it is Fitzgerald's portrait of the artist, suggests that Fitzgerald thinks of the artist himself as tragic. Yet next to Dreiser's and Conrad's skepticism, Fitzgerald's seems shallow, or evasive of the responsibility to form that Conrad acquits in leaving *Lord Jim* so open to the audience his novel evokes. For all its profound pessimism, *Lord Jim* is also a more hopeful novel than *The Great Gatsby*.

48. Northrop Frye, *Anatomy of Criticism* (Princeton, N.J.: Princeton University Press, 1957), 305.

Chapter 6

Jim, Marlow, and the Hero

You can detect the shape of a mangled idea and the shadow of an intention in the worst of one's work—and you make the best of it. You would almost persuade me that I exist. Almost!

JOSEPH CONRAD TO EDWARD GARNETT
November 24, 1899

In Marlow's account of his relationship with Lord Jim, he uses the phrase "one of us" nine different times.[1] Sometimes he uses the phrase so casually that it has the effect of a Homeric epithet—a quick, familiar, essential characterization that serves as a mnemonic device for the audience Marlow addresses. At another level, the repetition of "one of us" has the incremental effect of a ballad's refrain; each new use recalls the previous uses, but each new context gives the phrase a different slant. However apt these analogues are, the complexity of *Lord Jim* and Marlow's intention in using the phrase as he does suggest an apter analogue in the symbolist procedure I call the "progressive appositive." In this procedure, which Wallace Stevens uses quite often, a premise is set

1. Joseph Conrad, *Lord Jim*, ed. Thomas C. Moser (New York: W. W. Norton, 1968), 27, 48, 57, 65, 137, 201, 220, 253.

and then elaborated by appositions, but the elaboration is so extensive a process that the appositions finally seem not very apposite at all. The blackbird is the premise in Stevens' "Thirteen Ways of Looking at a Blackbird," but its meaning is so radically changed in each of the stanzas that the poem is less about the blackbird than it is a demonstration of the imagination's illimitability. The same can be said of "Sea Surface Full of Clouds," but perhaps the clearest short example of this process comes in "A Primitive Like an Orb," which begins with a consideration of "The essential poem at the centre of things." In the seventh stanza, the essential poem is the "central poem," "the poem of the whole," but by the end of the eighth stanza this poem has become something entirely unexpected.

VII

The central poem is the poem of the whole,
The poem of the composition of the whole,
The composition of blue sea and of green,
Of blue light and of green, as lesser poems,
And the miraculous multiplex of lesser poems,
Not merely into a whole, but a poem of
The whole, the essential compact of the parts,
The roundness that pulls tight the final ring

VIII

And that which in an altitude would soar,
A vis, a principle or, it may be,
The mediation of a principle,
Or else an inherent order active to be
Itself, a nature to its natives all
Beneficence, a repose, utmost repose,
The muscles of a magnet aptly felt;
A giant, on the horizon, glistening.

At this point, we have come a long way from the premise, "The central poem is the poem of the whole." In *Lord Jim*, by the time we hear Marlow say "one of us" on the final page, we will have also come a long way from his first use of it. And though the changes Marlow imposes on the phrase are not so abrupt as Stevens' changes, they are as thorough. For the phrase "one of us" is the focal point of Marlow's confession to the men on the veranda and the "privileged man"; and in the phrase, Marlow delivers the essence of his apology for Lord Jim, who has confessed to Marlow but cannot go home to enact his own apology. In elaborating the meaning of "one of us," Marlow tries to identify himself, Jim, and the community they both need. What gives the phrase its full complexity is that Marlow's identity and Jim's are so different, and Marlow's effort to reconcile them both into a single community is his attempt to redeem Jim from the tragic isolation and failure his heroism has led him to. More fully and more rigorously than *The Great Gatsby, Lord Jim* explores the different natures of the traditional and the modern hero, their equally difficult relationship to society, and the realistic novel's formal problems in presenting the traditional hero, who is a figure of action and ideals.[2] Moreover, Conrad sees the potential resolution of these problems in the confession, which is the dramatic basis of Marlow's entire narrative.

The first time Marlow uses "one of us," it is almost unnoticeable. On the same page, however, he uses it again as he describes Jim's appearance, his first impressions of Jim, his own ethical ideas of courage, and the kind of community Marlow once thought he naturally belonged to.

> I watched the youngster there. I liked his appearance, I knew his appearance; he came from the right place; he was one of us. He stood there for all the parentage of his kind, for men and women by no means clever or amusing, but whose very existence is based upon honest faith, and upon the instinct of courage. I don't mean military courage, or civil courage, or any special kind of courage. I mean just that inborn ability to look temptations straight in the face—a readiness

2. Conrad's literary attitude toward action is discussed by Edward W. Said, *Joseph Conrad and the Fiction of Autobiography* (Cambridge, Mass.: Harvard University Press, 1966), 43–44.

> unintellectual enough, goodness knows, but without pose—a power of resistance, don't you see, ungracious if you like, but priceless—an unthinking and blessed stiffness before the outward and inward terrors, before the might of nature, and the seductive corruption of men—backed by a faith invulnerable to the strength of facts, to the contagion of example, to the solicitation of ideas. Hang ideas! They are tramps, vagabonds, knocking at the back door of your mind, each taking a little of your substance, each carrying away some crumb of that belief in a few simple notions you must cling to if you want to live decently and would like to die easy![3]

At this point, Marlow's instinct for identification, his affinity for Jim and what Jim seems to embody, are nationalistic and racial. Jim is "one of us" first because of his looks: he is white, clean, British, middle-class. None of the other officers of the *Patna* looks so wholesome, and Marlow's first sighting of Jim takes place in the Far East. "One of us" will never lose this racial significance, but it will lose its nationalistic limitations as Marlow comes to understand that a personal identity cannot be so easily circumscribed. As he comes to understand the elusiveness of identity, he also redefines the community he needs for his own confirmation; and in doing this, he also relinquishes his notions about courage, which here are decidedly unromantic.[4] Beneath all these changes is the change that will take place in Marlow's attitude toward ideas. Despite himself, Marlow's notions are neither simple nor few, and his dismissal of ideas would be more convincing if his own ideas here were not so rich. In the next paragraph, he immediately admits his mistake about Jim, but he also admits his preference for a kind of stupidity or simplicity that his own mind and imagination will never allow him to have. "This has nothing to do with Jim,

3. Conrad, *Lord Jim*, 27.

4. See Georg Lukacs, *The Historical Novel*, trans. Hannah and Stanley Mitchell (Boston: Beacon Press, 1963), 39ff. Lukacs discusses Hegel's notion of "maintaining individuals" as the new heroes of realistic literature. These "maintaining individuals" embody qualities similar to the heroism Marlow sees in the middle-class parentage Jim supposedly represents.

directly; only he was outwardly so typical of that good, stupid kind we like to feel marching right and left of us in life, of the kind that is not disturbed by the vagaries of intelligence and the perversions of—of nerves, let us say. He was the kind of fellow you would, on the strength of his looks, leave in charge of the deck—figuratively and professionally speaking. I say I would, and I ought to know."[5]

Marlow now knows better than to insist on his prejudices, but these passages are an important background against which to judge the conversion he undergoes as a result of his encounter with Jim. Before he again claims Jim is "one of us," he explains something of this change in recounting his hospital interview with the *Patna's* chief engineer and the story of Big Brierly. The chief engineer's hallucinations are a brutal parody of Jim's vision and rationalizations, and Brierley's guilt and failure of courage are a standard against which Marlow's audience can measure Marlow's compassion and willingness to assume responsibility for Jim. Marlow does not present Brierly's story in a self-serving way. It comes up because it is part of Jim's story, part of Marlow's investigation of the nature of courage and moral responsibility, and part of the evidence that Jim's character and fate have compelled the attention of many people other than himself. This last motive is very important: for if Marlow is to justify Jim to the men on the veranda, he must also justify his interest in Jim by demonstrating that Jim's importance has been already acknowledged by others who have encountered him, whatever their reactions may have been.[6] In this respect, Brierley's reaction is crucial. It reinforces the racial aspect of the book because Brierly cannot endure witnessing Jim's humiliation in a country of dark-skinned men. But what is even more important is that Brierly's guilt also makes

5. Conrad, *Lord Jim*, 27.

6. John Palmer says, "And finally, all the Marlow tales involve such a variety of artifices tending to 'justify' Marlow as choral voice that the reader must suppose Conrad to have been deeply concerned in gaining the reader's trust for his inner narrator." *Joseph Conrad's Fiction* (Ithaca, N.Y.: Cornell University Press, 1968), 6.

him confront his own ego, his identity, as both Jim and Marlow must. If Brierly's suicide ironically reenacts Jim's jump from the *Patna* and foreshadows Jim's death, his implicit need for certitude complements Marlow's, who hoped to obtain from the chief engineer "some profound and redeeming cause, some merciful explanation, some convincing shadow of an excuse" against "the most obstinate ghost of man's creation . . . the doubt of the sovereign power enthroned in a fixed standard of conduct."[7] The absence of an absolute is what Brierly cannot tolerate, and his characterization embodies Conrad's insight into the guilt that harrows not the culpable but the impotent.

Without an absolute, Brierly can act only to kill himself. In the same circumstances, Marlow acts to have Jim's life. For his attachment to other men is, like Ishmael's, deeper than his need for an abstract certitude, and his recognition of the mysteries of individual identity is finally as strong as his own need for community. Therefore, despite the absurdity and threat of violence that almost spoil their first meeting outside the courtroom, Marlow persuades Jim to have dinner with him and, in the Malabar House, begins to listen to Jim's long confession. Still supported by the comforting aspect of Jim's appearance, Marlow sensibly recognizes Jim's readiness to renew himself and honors the ambiguities entailed in anyone's attempt to explain his own identity.

> A little wine opened Jim's heart and loosened his tongue. . . . He seemed to have buried somewhere the opening episode of our acquaintance. It was like a thing of which there would be no more question in this world. And all the time I had before me these blue, boyish eyes looking straight into mine, this young face, these capable shoulders, the open, bronzed forehead with a white line under the roots of clustering fair hair, this appearance appealing at sight to all my sympathies: this frank aspect, the artless smile, the youthful seriousness. He was of the right sort; he was one of us. He talked soberly, with a sort of composed unreserve, and with a

7. Conrad, *Lord Jim*, 31.

> quiet bearing that might have been the outcome of manly self-control, of impudence, of callousness, of a colossal unconsciousness, of a gigantic deception. Who can tell?[8]

Jim's appearance here is as powerful and important as Gatsby's when he delivers Nick the first, all-important smile. Although the novel, by its very nature, has taught us to look beyond appearances to the reality they may express but more often disguise, it is a mistake to dismiss the impact of appearances and their effect on so intimate an act as confession. A hero's looks, in particular, are often the initial manifestation of his charism. In discussing the hero in *Sincerity and Authenticity*, Lionel Trilling praises Jacques Barzun for "fixing upon the novel, the pedagogic genre *par excellence*, as the chief opponent of the heroic view of life." Yet in answering the question he then poses—"What is a hero?"—Trilling says:

> A good answer was given by the late Robert Warshow when, in an essay on Western films, he said: "A hero is one who looks like a hero." Warshow was saying essentially what Margaret Bieber had said in her book on the Greek theatre, that the hero is an actor. The two statements, especially Professor Bieber's, make it plain that the idea of the hero is only secondarily a moral idea; to begin with, it is no more so than the grace of a dancer is a moral idea. Nowadays our colloquial language makes the idea of the hero more or less coextensive with one of the moral qualities originally thought to be essential to it: "hero" is our word for a man who commits an approved act of unusual courage. But in the ancient literary conception of the hero, courage is only a single element, and although it is essential, it is not in itself definitive. It is virtually taken for granted in a man who is favoured by the gods, as the hero is presumed to be, and who is even endowed with certain traits of divinity. This favour of heritage of divinity

8. *Ibid*, 48.

> makes itself fully apparent. The dignity it confers on the man is not latent, to be revealed or discerned eventually, but is wholly manifest in word and deed, in physique and comportment. It announces and demonstrates itself. The hero is one who looks like a hero; the hero is an actor—he acts out his own high sense of himself.[9]

Much of what Marlow sees in Jim fits Trilling's description nicely. If Marlow can no longer believe in the favor of the old gods or in the unthinking community he once thought he belonged to, he can still respond to the mythical or vestigial signs of another order that do linger in certain individuals. Jim's high sense of himself Marlow will come to call "a sort of sublimated, idealised selfishness"; and the hero's divine heritage Marlow will redefine more naturalistically as Jim's harmony with his environment. "That was my last view of him—in a strong light, dominating, and yet in complete accord with his surroundings—with the life of the forests and with the life of men. I own that I was impressed, but I must admit to myself that after all this is not the lasting impression. He was protected by his isolation, alone of his own superior kind, in close touch with Nature, that keeps faith on such easy terms with her lovers."[10] Marlow's doubts, however, are constant; and because he doubts even his own perceptions, he also doubts the conventions behind an "approved act" of courage, the conventions embodied in the court's official understanding and definition of Jim. Throughout the novel, Marlow defines Jim's courage in terms of acts that others think cowardly or foolhardy: his refusal to flee, his willingness to stand trial, his constant readiness to prove himself again, his allegiance to communities that do not understand him. Understanding all this, Marlow also understands that Jim is an actor, but this recognition is precisely the source of Marlow's questions. For in Jim, the need to act is the need to overcome himself, to realize his integrity by means of a deliberate self-consciousness and will. So although he loves Jim's looks and is

9. Lionel Trilling, *Sincerity and Authenticity* (Cambridge, Mass.: Harvard University Press, 1972), 84–85.

10. Conrad, *Lord Jim*, 108, 107.

impressed by his performance, Marlow can still wonder whether his impression is produced by Jim's self-control or self-deception. In doing this, Marlow not only admits to his own limitations, he very quickly recasts the meaning of "one of us." Whoever accepts the import of this must also accept in himself the ambiguities Marlow sees in Jim.

Marlow has the advantage over Nick Carraway insofar as he is much older than Jim, whereas Nick is Gatsby's contemporary. This makes a real difference, not in the comparative quality of the two novels, but certainly in the quality of the two confessors' natural responses. Marlow is a fuller character, more focused than Nick; but he is still more ambivalent and more credible for his ambivalence, and more open to Jim and his own reactions, which makes him less hasty and self-protective. Consequently, he understands a number of important things very quickly. He knows that Jim "could never go home now" to face his father (whom the frame narrator has characterized as possessing "such certain knowledge of the Unknowable"); he also understands why Jim has to distinguish himself from the other white officers of the *Patna*: "He discovered at once a desire that I should not confound him with his partners in—in crime, let us call it. He was not one of them; he was altogether of another sort."[11] And Marlow is very conscious of all the difficulties in making a confession—the courage required, the embarrassment of asking for confirmation, and the terrible power of the conventions a confession must repudiate.

> I didn't know how much of it he believed himself. I didn't know what he was playing up to—if he was playing up to anything at all—and I suspect he did not know either; for it is my belief no man ever understands quite his own artful dodges to escape from the grim shadow of self-knowledge. I made no sound all the time he was wondering what he had better do after "that stupid inquiry was over."
>
> . . . .
>
> "It is all in being ready. I wasn't; not—not then. I

11. *Ibid.*, 49, 4.

> don't want to excuse myself; but I would like to explain—I would like somebody to understand—somebody—one person at least! You! Why not you?"
>
> It was solemn, and a little ridiculous, too, as they always are, those struggles of the individual trying to save from the fire his idea of what his moral identity should be, this precious notion of a convention, only one of the rules of the game, nothing more, but all the same so terribly effective by its assumption of unlimited power over natural instincts, by the awful penalties of its failure.[12]

Marlow's sympathetic insight is more convincing than his attempt to slight the "precious notion of a convention" as "only one of the rules of the game." But he makes the attempt because he is beginning to realize the extent of his own involvement. When he uses "one of us" again, he does so in the context of explaining his own struggle to maintain the convention of his "moral identity." The intimacy of any confession has its own power and makes its own demands, but what augments Jim's power here is a quality we will also see in Thomas Sutpen—an impersonality that seems to contradict the intimacy, an inner vision or self-absorption that almost denies the existence of the confessor.

> He was not speaking to me, he was only speaking before me, in a dispute with an invisible personality, an antagonist and inseparable partner of his existence—another possessor of his soul. These were issues beyond the competency of a court of inquiry; it was a subtle and momentous quarrel as to the true essence of life, and did not want a judge. He wanted an ally, a helper, an accomplice. I felt the risk I ran of being circumvented, blinded, decoyed, bullied, perhaps, into taking a definite part in a dispute impossible of decision if one had to be fair to all the phantoms in possession—to the reputable that had its claims and

12. *Ibid.*, 49, 50

> to the disreputable that had its exigencies. I can't explain to you who haven't seen him and who hear his words only at second hand the mixed nature of my feelings. It seemed to me I was being made to comprehend the Inconceivable—and I know of nothing to compare with the discomfort of such a sensation. I was made to look at the convention that lurks in all truth and on the essential sincerity of falsehood. He appealed to all sides at once—to the side turned perpetually to the light of day, and to that side of us which, like the other hemisphere of the moon, exists stealthily in perpetual darkness, with only a fearful ashy light falling at times on the edge. He swayed me. I own to it, I own up. The occasion was obscure, insignificant—what you will; a lost youngster, one in a million—but then he was one of us; an incident as completely devoid of importance as the flooding of an ant-heap, and yet the mystery of his attitude got hold of me as though he had been an individual in the forefront of his kind, as if the obscure truth involved were momentous enough to affect mankind's conception of itself.[13]

At this point Marlow stops to relight his cheroot, a gesture that is intended to give us pause too. We should remark first how powerfully this passage conveys the confessor's difficulty in hearing a confession of this kind, one so open that it addresses "the true essence of life" in a "dispute impossible of decision." Jephson is given no chance—because of his functional role and Clyde's character—even to experience this kind of doubt or intimidation; and Nick needs Gatsby so much, whether he can admit it or not, that the moment he raises his own doubts, he usually dismisses them in his hurry to define Gatsby's meaning. Marlow here is most like Michel's confessor in *The Immoralist*, who says he has been made to feel incriminated. Moreover, Marlow's audience on the veranda exerts a pressure on him that Nick never has to face as he converts Gatsby into literature. And, as Marlow enacts Jim's

13. *Ibid.*, 57.

struggle in his own, his confessors are intended to experience the same kind of compelling entailment that he has experienced in hearing Jim's confession. Most important, however, is that Marlow owns up to himself and to all the ideas he has about identity that have made him, almost against his will, such a perceptive audience. He can still try to diminish the occasion of Jim's confession as "obscure, insignificant"; he can say again that Jim is "one of us"; but he cannot avoid admitting that what is most compelling about Jim is that he seems to be an "individual in the forefront of his kind," whose identity involves an "obscure truth . . . momentous enough to affect mankind's conception of itself." This admission affects the meaning of "one of us" radically. Marlow first uses the phrase to define Jim simply, as part of an established community. But in admitting that Jim's identity contains a truth momentous enough to affect mankind's conception of itself, Marlow implicitly denies that original community's validity and stability and says, in effect, that Jim is not simply one of us but has by his actions redefined us, and we must now see ourselves as one of him if we are to understand ourselves. If so complex a book as *Lord Jim* can be epitomized in a single passage, this passage is it. Every issue involved in its use of the confessional form and in its examination of the hero is here.

Dorothy Van Ghent isolates these issues in her discussion of the problems contained in Jim's heroic nature. "We see the hero as an idealized human type (literally 'idealized' through his devotion to an idea of ethical action). . . . He is nevertheless an extraordinarily simplified *type*, divested of all psychological attributes but the very few that concretize his relationship to his idea. The simplification is classical; it is a simplification like that of Aeschylus' Orestes, possessed by the divine command, and like that of Sophocles' Oedipus, possessed by his responsibility for finding out the truth." This formula complements Trilling's sense of the divinely guaranteed hero who acts himself out; it also complements Northrop Frye's notion of the romance hero who is "idealized by revery"; and it applies to Gatsby. Van Ghent goes on, however, to define the problem of fitting such a classical, idealized type into the modern, realistic novel. "Thus there is nothing structurally internal to Jim's story that matches the positive moral relationship, in the ancient dramas, between the social destiny and the hero's destiny, the relationship that is presented concretely in the fact that the hero's agony is a saving social measure." Because the modern counterpart of the classical hero is disconnected from a natural community, the need for interpretation arises. "There are Jim's actions, which are concrete enough and simple as the concrete is simple. But the significance of the action is significance in the judgments of men, which are various; as soon as judgment is brought into the act, the act becomes not simple but protean."[14]

This problem of interpretation is not necessarily irresolvable, however, for Van Ghent has explained the formal and moral rationale of *Lord Jim*'s confessional impulse and method. Jim's need to confess is itself an ethical action by which he tries to explain his willingness to stand trial and his need to find another opportunity to prove his responsibility. Marlow's apology for Jim is also an ethical action, both on Jim's behalf and his own, by which he intends to identify himself and to create for both of them the community they need. Marlow may not be able to make Jim significant to "social destiny," but he tries to make Jim significant to the self-consciousness he would create in his audience.

Irving Howe explains the mode of Marlow's heroism, which is specifically different from the classical mode embodied in Jim, in his general statement about the modern hero. "The modern hero moves from the heroic deed to the heroism of consciousness, a heroism often available only in defeat. . . . And in consciousness he seeks those moral ends which the hero is traditionally said to have found through the deed."[15] Although Howe's words apply to Jim, who tries to redeem his failure of action in his confession to Marlow, they have a better application to the structure of *Lord*

14. Dorothy Van Ghent, *The English Novel: Form and Function* (New York: Harper and Row, 1953), 230, 232, 237.

15. Irving Howe, "The Idea of the Modern," in Irving Howe (ed.), *Literary Modernism* (Greenwich, Conn.: Fawcett Publications, 1967), 36.

Jim and to Marlow's role. *Lord Jim* moves from deed to consciousness in moving from the frame narrator's account of Jim to Marlow's confessional apology for him. And it is in his conscious understanding of Jim that Marlow tries to fix Jim's significance, despite the ambiguities, and to define himself as both Jim's advocate and the representative of the white community that can validate Jim in a way that the community of Patusan cannot.

Conrad, like Fitzgerald and Faulkner after him, obviously wants to preserve in Jim as much as he can of the traditional heroic figure, the man of deeds. His skepticism of the deed itself and his sense of the novel's formal imperatives, however, lead him to repudiate the popular, anachronistic, "light holiday literature" from which Jim initially derives his appetite for heroism.[16] So Conrad turns to the confessional form to give both his heroes their due, to give them both a mode of ethical action by which they can define themselves more convincingly. In doing so, he provides an example of Victor Brombert's claim that while the traditional hero's definition is primarily entailed in his relationships with the supernatural order and the social group, the modern hero's relation to himself is his most crucial problem. "A greater psychological sophistication accompanies an age of doubt and demythification. The rift between thought and action, the inner split of personality, the subject-object relationship in the recesses of the mind, the peculiar mirror-disease, are widespread manifestations of an identity crisis. . . . The underlying tensions of moral and psychological relativism, the questioning of the political and cosmic orders, tend to discredit all notions of *being*, laying stress on the all-important *becoming* and forcing man into a permanent search, or rather a permanent creation, of his own image."[17] As no other form quite does, the confession allows the speaker to explore his relationship to himself and, with its intrinsic orientation toward the future, also allows him to engender his own becoming.

16. Conrad, *Lord Jim*, 4.

17. Victor Brombert, "The Idea of the Hero," in Victor Brombert (ed.), *The Hero in Literature* (Greenwich, Conn.: Fawcett Publications, 1969), 13.

Jim pursues this self-confrontation and self-creation on Patusan, but he never does it more intensely than he does in confronting Marlow as he tries to complete his confession.

> "Don't you believe me?" he cried. "I swear! . . . Confound it! You got me here to talk, and . . . You must! . . . you said you would believe." "Of course I do, " I protested in a matter-of-fact tone which produced a calming effect. "Forgive me," he said. "Of course I wouldn't have talked to you about all this if you had not been a gentleman. I ought to have known . . . I am—I am—a gentleman, too . . ." "Yes, yes," I said hastily. He was looking me squarely in the face and withdrew his gaze slowly. "Now you understand why I didn't after all . . . didn't go out in that way. I wasn't going to be frightened at what I had done. And, anyhow, if I had stuck to the ship I would have done my best to be saved."[18]

In that word "gentleman," we hear an echo of the Underground Man, who uses the word with as much irony as Jim does sincerity. The word contains an established order of value and decorum by which Jim appeals to Marlow as earnestly as he has appealed to his audience with the ideas contained in "one of us." Marlow explains an aspect of that order when he explains in the silence after Jim's pause: "Don't you see what I mean by the solidarity of the craft? I was aggrieved against him, as though he had cheated me—me!—of a splendid opportunity to keep the illusion of my beginnings, as though he had robbed our common life of the last spark of its glamour." But with gentlemanly restraint, Marlow tries to mollify Jim, who, to his credit, will not be mollified.

> "And so you cleared out—at once.
>
> "Jumped," he corrected me incisively. "Jumped—mind!" he repeated, and I wondered at the evident but obscure intention. "Well, yes! Perhaps I could not see then. But I had plenty of time and any amount of light in that boat. And I could think, too.

18. Conrad, *Lord Jim*, 80.

> Nobody would know, of course, but this did not make it any easier for me. You've got to believe that, too. I did not want all this talk. . . . No . . . Yes . . . I won't lie . . . I wanted it: it is the very thing I wanted—there. Do you think you or anybody could have made me if I . . . I am—I am not afraid to tell. And I wasn't afraid to think either. I looked it in the face. I wasn't going to run away. At first—at night, if it hadn't been for those fellows I might have . . . No! by heavens; I was not going to give them that satisfaction. They had done enough. They made up a story, and believed it for all I know. But I knew the truth, and I would live it down—alone, with myself. I wasn't going to give in to such a beastly unfair thing. What did it prove after all? I was confoundedly cut up. Sick of life—to tell you the truth; but what would have been the good to shirk it—in—in—that way? That was not the way. I believe—I believe it would have—it would have ended—nothing."
>
> He had been walking up and down, but with the last word he turned short at me.
>
> "What do *you* believe?" he asked with violence. A pause ensued, and suddenly I felt myself overcome by a profound and hopeless fatigue, as though his voice had startled me out of a dream of wandering through empty spaces whose immensity had harassed my soul and exhausted my body.
>
> " . . . Would have ended nothing," he muttered over me obstinately, after a little while. "No! the proper thing was to face it out—alone—for myself—wait for another chance—find out."[19]

Jim gets his other chance on Patusan and has his need for responsibility acknowledged, and almost satisfied, in the Bugis' need for him. But he cannot, in spite of this, completely relinquish his need for Marlow and, through Marlow, his even deeper need for an attachment to the community from which he originates. In the

19. *Ibid.*, 80–81.

penultimate installment of his confession, Jim tries to stop talking about himself in the same breath in which he reaffirms his need to maintain connection with the white world beyond Patusan. " 'No. I can't say—enough. Never. I must go on, go on for ever holding up my end, to feel sure that nothing can touch me. I must stick to their belief in me to feel safe and to—to' . . . he cast about for a word, seemed to look for it on the sea . . . 'to keep in touch with' . . . his voice sank suddenly to a murmur . . . 'with those whom, perhaps, I shall never see anymore. With—with—you, for instance.' "[20] Jim's scrupulous precision, his dependence and need to be independent, his insistence and abashment are as poignant and moving as Augustine's; and his painful honesty, whatever its element of self-delusion, is more convincing evidence of his heroism (and the act of courage we now most approve) than is his political effect on Patusan and the legendary maneuver by which he gets the guns up the hill.

Marlow himself undergoes self-confrontations as exacerbating as Jim'; and because he does not have an outlet in action like the one that Jim has on Patusan, his action consists of confronting other audiences. Many of these confrontations are difficult for several reasons, but Marlow's most intense moment of guilt, self-exposure, and doubt comes in his account of trying to get Jim off the hook, being refused, and having to face his own cowardice, the root of his ego and the proof of Jim's moral superiority.

> Our communion in the night was uncommonly like a last vigil with a condemned man. He was guilty, too. He was guilty—as I had told myself repeatedly, guilty and done for; nevertheless, I wished to spare him the mere detail of a formal execution. I don't pretend to explain the reasons of my desire—I don't think I could; but if you haven't got a sort of notion by this time, then I must have been very obscure in my narrative, or you too sleepy to seize upon the sense of my words. I don't defend my morality. There was no morality in the impulse which induced me to lay before him Brierly's plan of

20. *Ibid.*, 203.

> evasion—I may call it—in all its primitive simplicity. There were the rupees—absolutely ready in my pocket and very much at his service. . . . If he had not enlisted my sympathies he had done better for himself—he had gone to the very fount and origin of that sentiment, he had reached the secret sensibility of my egoism. I am concealing nothing from you, because were I to do so my action would appear more unintelligible than any man's action has the right to be, and—in the second place—to-morrow you will forget my sincerity along with the other lessons of the past. In this transaction, to speak grossly and precisely, I was the irreproachable man; but the simple intentions of my immorality were defeated by the moral simplicity of the criminal. No doubt he was selfish, too, but his selfishness had a higher origin, a more lofty aim. I discovered that, say what I would, he was eager to go through the ceremony of execution; and I didn't say much, for I felt in that argument his youth would tell against me heavily: he believed where I had already ceased to doubt.[21]

In this passage, which defines Jim's own idea of himself—his "moral simplicity" and the selfishness with the loftier aim—it is important to note that Marlow does not say Jim is "one of us." It is also important to notice Marlow's rare impatience with his audience. His honesty about his doubts and reactions, his lack of pretense that he finally understands Jim, and his willingness to confront everyone make it unnecessary for him to define the antipathetic audience, the "strange children," as explicitly as other confessional speakers must. The antagonists of *Lord Jim* are fully dramatized in Brierly, the French lieutenant, Chester, Gentleman Brown, the privileged man, and even, to a certain extent, Jewel. In Marlow's account to the men on the veranda, he does not often have to work out with them what he has worked out with these other characters. Instead, Conrad can offer those dramatic incidents as proof of Marlow's integrity, the guarantee that Marlow

21. *Ibid.*, 92–93.

has tested his ideas of Jim against all comers, and as further evidence that Marlow is not alone in thinking Jim important or representative.

Chester is somewhat less important than Brierly because of his cynicism and selfishness. His plan to use Jim to supervise the island of guano is a parody of Stein's arrangement to give Jim the chance he needs on Patusan. But Marlow has little trouble seeing through Chester. He has more difficulty with the French lieutenant, who stayed aboard the *Patna* for thirty hours as it was being towed back to port, for the French lieutenant has led his life according to that standard of courage that is "backed by a faith invulnerable to the strength of facts, to the contagion of example, to the solicitation of ideas." Marlow says he is "one of those steady, reliable men who are the raw material of great reputations, one of those uncounted lives that are buried without drums and trumpets under the foundations of monumental successes." Moreover, the French lieutenant dresses like a priest in "threadbare black *soutane*" and listens to Marlow's confession "looking more priest-like than ever." He does not, however, offer Marlow much satisfaction, for he does not take "a lenient view"; he sees little hope for Jim's redemption, since he has lost his honor. When he refuses to continue their conversation and rises from the table in the cafe, Marlow's frustration is acute. "Hang the fellow! he had pricked the bubble. The blight of futility that lies in wait for men's speeches had fallen upon our conversation, and made it a thing of empty sounds."[22]

Although Marlow meets the French lieutenant after Jim has gone to Patusan, the episode's position in Marlow's narrative establishes it as a prelude to Marlow's trip to see Stein. Jim's story tells of his search for the proper opportunity in which to prove his courage and to act out his idea of his character; Marlow's story is his search for an audience as sympathetic and understanding as he has been. In Stein alone, perhaps, he finds such a confessor. "I desired to confide my difficulty to him because he was one of the

22. *Ibid.*, 27, 87, 85, 88, 90.

most trustworthy men I had ever known." But Stein's other credentials are equally important. In his youth he had been a great adventurer and there is no single episode in the novel as romantically satisfying as his capture of the butterfly. He has become a successful merchant, he is "a naturalist of some distinction," his nature is "upright and indulgent," and he possesses "an intrepidity of spirit and a physical courage that could have been called reckless had it not been like a natural function of the body—say good digestion, for instance—completely unconscious of itself."[23] Stein is obviously very unlike the men on the veranda, in no way "one of us." He is immediately able to identify Jim's romanticism; to define his problem as "How to be!"; and to make good his orphic advice of immersing in the destructive element by commissioning Jim as his agent on Patusan, where he knows Jim will have not only another chance but also another father figure in Doramin. Marlow is less satisfied by the opportunity Stein gives Jim than Jim is because of the new question Stein raises in Marlow's mind. Jim is a romantic, Marlow sees that "no one could be more romantic than" Stein himself, but Marlow is left with the uneasy feeling that he is a romantic too. The issue of romanticism he confronts directly the next time he insists that Jim is "one of us."

Chapter 21 closes the first half of *Lord Jim*; in Chapter 22, Jim leaves for Patusan. Marlow's send-off is a long paragraph that runs for almost three pages and contains many of his deepest feelings. He begins by admitting that he may have been eager to "dispose" of Jim because Marlow was then about to go home and to all that home represents of the certain, the immutable, the natural. "I think it is the lonely, without a fireside or an affection they may call their own, those who return not to a dwelling but to the land itself, to meet its disembodied, eternal, and unchangeable spirit—it is those who understand best its severity, its saving power, the grace of its secular right to our fidelity, to our obedience. Yes! few of us understand, but we all feel it though, and I say *all* without exception, because those who do not feel do not

23. *Ibid.*, 112, 123.

count." Marlow needs the land's severity and saving power as an escape from all the uncertainty and turbulence of his relationship with Jim; home and the land constitute a mode of certitude that Marlow finds nowhere else. He says: "I cannot say I had ever seen him distinctly—not even to this day, after I had my last view of him; but it seemed to me that the less I understood the more I was bound to him in the name of that doubt which is the inseparable part of our knowledge. I did not know so much more about myself." These doubts about himself lead Marlow to confess his deepest fear at that time: that he would run into Jim again, be "waylaid by a blear-eyed, swollen-faced, besmirched loafer, with no soles to his canvas shoes, and with a flutter of rags about the elbows, who, on the strength of old acquaintance, would ask for a loan of five dollars." He goes on:

> That, to tell you the truth, was the only danger I could see for him and for me; but I also mistrusted my want of imagination. It might even come to something worse; in some way it was beyond my powers of fancy to foresee. He wouldn't let me forget how imaginative he was, and your imaginative people swing farther in any direction, as if given a longer scope of cable in the uneasy anchorage of life. They do. They take a drink, too. It may be I was belittling him by such a fear. How could I tell? Even Stein could say no more than that he was romantic. I only knew he was one of us. And what business had he to be romantic? I am telling you so much about my own instinctive feelings and bemused reflections because there remains so little to be told of him. He existed for me, and after all it is only through me that he exists for you.[24]

Marlow's fear does underestimate Jim; by his mistrust of his own imagination, he also underestimates himself. Yet, he tries to shift this failure of imagination to his audience, attacking them again for lacking the imagination he has just claimed he lacks himself.

24. *Ibid.*, 136, 135, 137.

> My last words about Jim shall be few. I affirm he had achieved greatness; but the thing would be dwarfed in the telling, or rather in the hearing. Frankly, it is not my words that I mistrust, but your minds. I could be eloquent were I not afraid you fellows had starved your imagination to feed your bodies. I do not mean to be offensive; it is respectable to have no illusions—and safe—and profitable—and dull. Yet you, too, in your time must have known the intensity of life, that light of glamour created in the shock of trifles, as amazing as the glow of sparks struck from a cold stone—and as short-lived, alas![25]

Marlow's assault on his audience is perfectly placed; it expresses his own doubts more convincingly than it defines their limitations; and it is a rhetorical ploy on Conrad's part to try to persuade the reader that he should be more imaginative than the men on the veranda in appreciating the significance of the story to come. For what ensues is the long narrative of Jim's early career on Patusan—jumping the fence, getting the guns up the hill, establishing peace and order among the native factions. However important these deeds are to Jim himself, they seem less enthralling to the modern reader, like Albert Guerard, who finds the exploits tiresome, a little unconvincing, and irrelevant to what Guerard calls "the essential Jim."[26] Conrad works as hard as he can to write a satisfying adventure story, and he sets up a symmetry of relationships that links the two halves of the novel together. But what is missing from the second half, until Marlow himself arrives on Patusan, is the intensity of the confrontations that make the first half so compelling. The adventure story of Jim is the material of

25. *Ibid.*, 138.

26. Albert J. Guerard, *Conrad the Novelist* (Cambridge, Mass.; Harvard University Press, 1958), 168. However, Conrad's romanticism and his belief in the romantic conventions of adventure narrative are persuasively argued for by David Thorburn, *Conrad's Romanticism* (New Haven, Conn.: Yale University Press, 1974). Thorburn is also alert to the tension between self-consciousness and the need for community that informs romantic literature in general and *Lord Jim* in particular.

light holiday literature, and Marlow himself has very little to do but report Jim's adventures. In the second half, Marlow's role as apologist and interpreter remains in abeyance; and what this demonstrates is that the most convincing basis of Jim's heroism is not his deeds but his character, the looks and personality that compel Marlow to see in him the "obscure truth . . . momentous enough to affect mankind's conception of itself." Therefore Jim's most important act of heroism is his confession, which changes Marlow's mind about the meaning of human nature and leads him to tell Jim's story in order to justify his own conversion.

In narrating Jim's career on Patusan, Marlow goes a very long time without saying Jim is "one of us," for Tuan Jim at this point is clearly not. Marlow's most interesting statement along the way is his attempt to define himself as "one of us." "I suppose you think that I, too, am romantic, but it is a mistake." It is hard to accept this disclaimer except as further evidence of Marlow's need to simplify complexities. When he next says Jim is "one of us," his remark is also a simplification and essentially racial. It comes in the context of Marlow's last impression of the people he has met on Patusan; he mentions Doramin and his wife Tunku Allang, Dain Waris, Jewel, Tamb' Itam, and Cornelius. "I am certain of them," Marlow says. "They exist as if under an enchanter's wand. But the figure round which all these are grouped—that one lives, and I am not certain of him. No magician's wand can immobilise him under my eyes. He is one of us."[27]

The mystery Marlow sees in Jim's identity is not a quality he has originally ascribed to the men on the veranda, to the audience he has tried so hard to simplify in the phrase "one of us." This mystery is, however, a quality Jewel also recognizes in Jim, and it is the source of her doubts and the desperate questions she asks of Marlow as he is about to leave Patusan forever. Neither Marlow nor Jewel makes a confession, but their scene together has all the personal intensity that the narrative of Jim's adventure career has lacked. Both of them also transfer their own skepticism and frus-

27. Conrad, *Lord Jim*, 172, 201.

tration onto the other: Marlow says Jim will not leave Patusan for the white world "because he is not good enough"; Jewel responds by calling Marlow a liar. Jim himself tries to allay the doubts in the air by saying in his last conversation with Marlow: "I shall be faithful . . . I shall be faithful."[28] Faithful to what? To his idea of himself, to the native community that needs him, to Marlow and the white community Marlow represents, or to Jewel?

The irresolution with which this section of the novel ends (at the conclusion of Chapter 35) leaves the men on the veranda drifting off, incapable of comment or response. This irresolution is one of the reasons Marlow must complete his narrative to the privileged man in the letter he writes "more than two years later." Also behind the letter are Jim's own last attempt to complete his confession in the letter he tries to write from Patusan and the counterconfession of Gentleman Brown that Marlow has the extraordinary fortune to hear from Brown's deathbed. Marlow does not know to whom Jim addresses his letter, if to anyone, but he assumes the responsibility of finishing for Jim. In doing so, he assumes an "artistic" responsibility in his decision to relate it as though he had been an eyewitness.

> My information was fragmentary, but I've fitted the pieces together, and there is enough of them to make an intelligible picture. I wonder how he would have related it himself. He has confided so much in me that at times it seems as though he must come in presently and tell the story in his own words, in his careless yet feeling voice, with his offhand manner, a little puzzled, a little bothered, a little hurt, but now and then by a word or a phrase giving one of those glimpses of his very own self that were never any good for purposes of orientation.[29]

Marlow's decision here restores him to the apologetic role he could not play in narrating Jim's early career on Patusan; and this, as much as anything he says, gives these final chapters their power.

28. *Ibid.*, 194, 203.
29. *Ibid.*, 205, 208–209.

But what saves Marlow from converting Jim into literature is the audience he chooses and addresses directly.

In choosing a specific audience, Marlow continues his own confession, which he must do to satisfy his irresolution about Jim and about his own identity. In choosing the privileged man as his correspondent, Marlow deliberately confronts the most established, the most representative of the "strange children." The privileged man embodies the racism, the skepticism, and the notion of community most antithetical to the mode of heroism embodied in Jim. Marlow says to him:

> You alone have showed an interest in him that survived the telling of his story, though I remember well you would not admit he had mastered his fate. You prophesied for him the disaster of weariness and of disgust with acquired honor, with the self-appointed task, with the love sprung from pity and youth. You had said you knew so well "that kind of thing," its illusory satisfaction, its unavoidable deception. You said also—I call to mind—that "giving your life up to them" (*them* meaning all of mankind with skins brown, yellow, or black in colour) "was like selling your soul to a brute." You contended that "that kind of thing" was only endurable and enduring when based on the firm conviction in the truth of ideas racially our own, in whose name are established the order, the morality of an ethical progress. "We want its strength at our backs," you had said. "We want a belief in its necessity and its justice, to make a worthy and conscious sacrifice of our lives. Without it the sacrifice is only a forgetfulness, the way of offering is no better than the way to perdition." In other words, you maintained that we must fight in the ranks or our lives can't count. Possibly! You ought to know—be it said without malice—you who have rushed into one or two places single-handed and came out cleverly, without singeing your wings. The point, however, is that of all mankind Jim had no dealings but with himself, and the question is whether

> at the last he had not confessed to a faith mightier than the laws of order and progress.[30]

Marlow's integrity is impressive: not only does he summarize the strongest case of the loyal opposition, he responds with his most emphatic affirmation of Jim's heroic identity, despite the fact that he couches it as a question and says immediately, "I affirm nothing." These words themselves, however, do affirm Marlow's openness, the skepticism that keeps his sympathy from becoming automatic or strident, his deep involvement nonetheless, and his courage in refusing to stop short. Of course, behind these words is also Marlow's need, which he expresses with an unanticipated pathos in his last rhetorical questions to his confessor.

> He goes away from a living woman to celebrate his pitiless wedding with a shadowy ideal of conduct. Is he satisfied—quite, now, I wonder? We ought to know. He is one of us—and have I not stood up once, like an evoked ghost, to answer for his eternal constancy? Was I so very wrong after all? Now he is no more, there are days when the reality of his existence comes to me with an immense, with an overwhelming force; and yet upon my honour there are moments, too, when he passes from my eyes like a disembodied spirit astray amongst the passions of his earth, ready to surrender himself faithfully to the claim of his own world of shades.[31]

Marlow's loneliness at the very end seems to diminish the eager optimism of *Lord Jim*'s epigraph from Novalis: "It is certain my conviction gains infinitely, the moment another soul will believe in it." However much Marlow's belief has confirmed Jim, it cannot resolve the final question of Jim's identity, which he opened again and closed in his final sacrifice. We are left at the end of *Lord Jim* with the same question we are left with at the end of *Red and Black*: Is the death of this young man really necessary? The questions Marlow asks about himself are somewhat easier. Yes, he has stood up to answer for Jim and his "eternal constancy."

30. *Ibid.*, 205–206.
31. *Ibid.*, 253.

No, he was not "so very wrong after all." But this question remains: Were the privileged man to respond with these answers, would Marlow be satisfied? The question is unanswerable. Marlow's opinion of Jim is not at stake; nor is the fidelity of his apology and performance. His own identity is the question, and it does not answer to the binary resolutions of yes and no.

The great strength of *Lord Jim* is that it never becomes so simple as Marlow would like, but will not allow, his own narrative to be. And Conrad himself, as nobly as Marlow, confesses to the problems that the openness of *Lord Jim* has caused him, his own doubts, his unrequitedness, and his simple upset that not everyone has accepted Jim as "one of us."[32] Conrad makes his brief confession in the Author's Note he wrote more than sixteen years after the novel's completion. He takes up first some fairly trivial questions about the novel's origin, growth, and the verisimilitude of Marlow's long monologue. What is really on his mind, however, is the report from a friend that a lady in Italy found the novel morbid, which is one way of attacking Jim's heroism and Marlow's refusal of simple explanations. Addressing the note to "my readers"—the lady is clearly his "strange child"—Conrad sounds as open-minded to other opinions as Marlow is, as speculative and as apologetic. But he is also firm.

> I wonder whether she was European at all? In any case, no Latin temperament would have perceived anything morbid in the acute consciousness of lost honour. Such a consciousness may be wrong, or it may be right, or it may be condemned as artificial; and, perhaps, my Jim is not a type of wide commonness. But I can safely assure

32. Gustav Morf argues, on psychological grounds, that *Lord Jim* is Conrad's own confession, made out of his guilt at having left Poland. See *The Polish Heritage of Joseph Conrad* (London: Sampson Low, Marston, 1930), 149–66. Morf's argument is somewhat mechanical and allegorical. His conclusions, however, have been accepted by Jocelyn Baines, *Joseph Conrad: A Critical Biography* (New York: McGraw-Hill, 1960), 254–55. A more temperate argument is made by Leo Gurko, *Joseph Conrad: Giant in Exile* (New York: Macmillan, 1962). Gurko recognizes Conrad's need for a community, but he does not oversimplify this need's immediate effect on *Lord Jim.* See also Eloise Knapp Hay, "Lord Jim: From Sketch to Novel," *Comparative Literature,* XII (Fall, 1960), 289–309.

> my readers that he is not the product of coldly perverted thinking. He is not a figure of Northern Mists either. One sunny morning in the commonplace surroundings of an Eastern roadstead, I saw his form pass by—appealing —significant—under a cloud—perfectly silent. Which is as it should be. It was for me, with all the sympathy of which I was capable, to seek fit words for his meaning. He was "one of us."

Conrad's admission that Jim may not be a "type of wide commonness" but nonetheless "one of us," and the earnest testament of his own good faith make him sound a lot like Marlow; but his words do not allow an easier resolution than Marlow's words. The other expatriate novelist of the nineteenth century who wrote under a pseudonym and loved the personal passion of the Latin temperament is Stendhal, whose vision of his contemporary society was so pessimistic he consigned himself to the more enlightened community of posterity. Stendhal's commitment to the heroic personality was as strong as Conrad's; his narrative method is, in its own way, as brilliant; but it is also more self-defensive, more manipulative of both character and reader, less open to response. As Gide says: "In Stendhal no phrase evokes the one after it or takes life from the preceding one. Each one stands perpendicular to the fact or idea."[33] Conrad's method, however, his characterization of his narrator, and his use of the confessional form not only invite a response, but encourage it, perhaps even demand it.

What we do with the unresolved tension at the end of *Lord Jim*, which Conrad dramatizes so emphatically in the plea in Marlow's questions, is the fulfillment of the novel's confessional form. Of course, we are not free to cross the aesthetic boundary to respond to Marlow, contend with or ratify his judgments, console him in his loss, or confirm his virtue. We are, however, much freer at the end of *Lord Jim* than we are at the end of *The Great Gatsby*. We have seen Jim through the eyes of the neutral frame narrator, we have had an almost unmediated view of his career on Patusan, and we have had the example of Marlow's refusal to seek neat conclusions. We have, in other words, not only the self-

33. Quoted in Stendhal, *Red and Black*, ed. and trans. Robert M. Adams (New York: W. W. Norton, 1969), 563.

consciousness that open-ended forms create in the reader, we also have the dignity and autonomy that Marlow allows the privileged man. Beyond this we have, in the precedent of Marlow's letter, the license to "fictionalize" that is necessary if we are to complete for ourselves the meaning of the phrase "one of us." W. H. Auden says that we do not read great books so much as they read us. As we decide for ourselves exactly what "one of us" means, we are each deciding who we are, and this is exactly what confessors must do as they respond in good faith to confessions like Jim's and Marlow's.

Chapter 7

Quentin and Shreve, Sutpen and Bon

What is the use of talking,
and there is no end of talking,
There is no end of things in the heart.

EZRA POUND
"Exile's Letter"

When Thomas Sutpen first confides in General Compson, as they hunt down the French architect dragooned to build Sutpen's house, he begins the first of the confessions that inform *Absalom, Absalom!* Sutpen chooses Compson, rather than someone like Goodhue Coldfield, for Compson's status in the Jefferson community, and Sutpen makes his confession in two installments. The first installment has no particular confessional urgency; it sounds like the campfire conversation of two men who do not yet know each other well. Sutpen speaks of his past, but he does not feel the need to justify himself that he feels thirty years later in Compson's office. Rosa Coldfield's confession seems to begin in a similar way when she summons Quentin Compson, supposedly for instruction in the Sutpen mysteries, but delivers her own confession and its fierce apology instead. Then Quentin's confession begins as though it were going to be meditative reminiscences on the characters out of his past. Sutpen's confession and Rosa's have obvious analogues: his in Lord Jim's, hers in the Underground Man's. Quentin's confession is different, for he does not seem to talk explicitly about himself at all. He talks principally about Sutpen and also about Sutpen's family and Rosa. Still, much of what he says comes not from his own firsthand experience, but from previous conversations with his grandfather and father. In his confession Quentin plays something like the role of Nick or Marlow —the narrator-apologist who relates the story of another man whose identity has an important, extrapersonal significance and who is the kind of character we commonly designate as heroic. But Quentin does not feel so strongly as Nick and Marlow the need to apologize for himself or Sutpen, because Sutpen, unlike Jim or Gatsby, is a given. He is clearly involved in the historical fate of a specific community and there is no doubt in Quentin's mind that Sutpen is "one of us." Quentin's questions are, Who are we? and, therefore, Who am I? Faulkner tells us immediately that Quentin, because of his immersion in his community's history and his consciousness of the historical determinants of his identity, is not "a being, an entity" but a "commonwealth."[1] So, to understand himself, Quentin must understand the commonwealth he embodies. This need leads him to seek a confessor from outside that community—Shreve McCannon.

A Canadian, Shreve enters the novel and its ambiance from about as far away as possible, and he hears Quentin's story as the snow falls outside their room in Harvard Yard. If he is an unlikely audience to the legend of Thomas Sutpen, he is even more unlikely in his eventual role as narrator and apologist. Yet Shreve is eventually forced to respond and to enact his own part in the process of understanding. He is not merely Quentin's straw man or foil; he is *Absalom, Absalom!*'s "privileged man," the reader's model, the representative of the community that is the end of the

1. William Faulkner, *Absalom, Absalom!* (New York: Modern Library, 1954), 12.

novel's confessional intention and form.[2] What distinguishes Shreve is that he is allowed to talk back.

David Goldknopf has said that in first-person narratives, as distinguished from third-person narratives, someone inside the book is talking to someone outside the book.[3] Goldknopf's admirable enthusiasm for this kind of immediacy is a little misleading, however, for I think that most of us feel directly addressed by certain third-person narrators who, in moments of particular intensity, seem to speak in the voice of the author himself. Charles Dickens' *Bleak House* is full of such moments, as are George Eliot's *Middlemarch* and Thomas Hardy's novels. At one moment in *Red and Black* Stendhal breaks through his narrator's voice to talk about himself and his own relation to Julien: "This glimpse of the *sublime* restored to Julien all the energy that the specter of M. Chelan had dissipated. He was still very young; but in my opinion, he was a fine plant. Instead of treading the common path from softness to cunning, like most men, advancing years would have given him easy access to a fund of generous feeling; he would have overcome his morbid mistrust. . . . But what is the point of these vain suppositions?"[4] This is a very different kind of intrusion from those in which Stendhal interrupts his narrative to defend his method, the political aspects of his story, and Mathilde's verisimilitude. Someone inside the novel is talking to someone outside the novel, but the crucial difference is this: we do not feel the need to respond to Dickens, Eliot, or Stendhal. However personal the

2. The earlier critics who do not dismiss or minimize Shreve's role are Olga W. Vickery, *The Novels of William Faulkner: A Critical Interpretation* (Rev. ed.; Baton Rouge: Louisiana State University Press, 1964) and Hyatt Waggoner, *William Faulkner: From Jefferson to the World* (Lexington: University of Kentucky Press, 1959). Their chapters on *Absalom, Absalom!* have greatly influenced my understanding of the novel. Two other readings sympathetic to Shreve's role are Joseph W. Reed, Jr., *Faulkner's Narrative* (New Haven, Conn.: Yale University Press, 1973), and Virginia V. Hlavsa, "The Vision of the Advocate in *Absalom, Absalom!*," *Novel*, VIII (Fall, 1974), 51–70.

3. David Goldknopf, *The Life of the Novel* (Chicago: University of Chicago Press, 1972), 33.

4. Stendhal, *Red and Black*, ed. and trans. Robert M. Adams (New York: W. W. Norton, 1969), 371.

voice of the author becomes, there is still a degree of formality that keeps us in our place. Third-person narratives are one-way streets; many first-person narratives, especially those as open as *Lord Jim*, are not. And confessional novels in particular work to elicit from the reader the desire to talk back. Talking back to Marlow is conceivable in a way that talking back to the narrator of Conrad's *Nostromo* is not.

We cannot, of course, make our response on the same ontological ground from which it is elicited. By means of the privileged man, Conrad recognizes the tension this creates, and therefore encourages us to talk to ourselves with something like Marlow's own scrupulous care and sympathy. Faulkner takes a step beyond Conrad, however, by allowing Shreve to respond and by making that response a model of the response he expects from us. *Absalom, Absalom!* works to transcend the limits of its own art by positing community as a higher value than art itself. This intention to transcend art is not an uncommon motive among the greatest modern writers, but it is also the essential paradox behind the difficulty of the techniques they use to surpass their own technique. Shreve is a perfect case in point. His participation in Quentin's confession is finally achieved by the power of his own "artistic" imagination, the special creativity of his sympathy. Shreve and Quentin together develop the kind of community that surpasses social roles and political orders to accommodate more urgent human needs, and their way of talking to each other even "overpasses" the personal limits of their experience and knowledge. Shreve's active role not only supports Quentin and confirms his effort to understand Sutpen and himself, it also gives to Charles Bon a place and an identity Bon never has in his own life. Shreve begins as something of Bon's counterpart and ends as Bon's apologist—as the only voice Bon has, in fact. Shreve is in no way making his own confession, but because of him the confessional community of *Absalom, Absalom!* has a principle of renewal, extension, and continuity that is shared by no other confessional novel we have examined.

Sutpen first turns to General Compson because Compson is

more established—a gentleman, later an officer, and a lawyer. Without saying so, Sutpen thinks of himself as a kind of convert, but he has converted to a social institution much less clearly defined and ritualized than, say, the church Augustine enters. In 1834, Sutpen is something of an arriviste who nonetheless talks to Compson as an equal. He tells Compson then of his youth, his decisive confrontation with the "monkey nigger" (which is, in effect, the beginning of his conversion), and his career on Haiti. Later in 1864, when he is more firmly planted in Jefferson, Sutpen can confess the nature and purpose of his design and his reasons for setting Eulalia Bon aside to marry Ellen Coldfield. By this time, in the midst of the war, Sutpen's design has crucial social and historical implications; in trying to justify himself, he is implicitly trying to justify an experience representative of the entire South.[5]

Whether or not Sutpen sees this, General Compson does, and he sees even more in the odd, revealing impersonality of Sutpen's delivery. Sutpen's habitual bombast is a social affectation; it is not the kind of personal rhetoric that is essential to confession or fosters sympathy, but it is a style apparently intended to suggest a gentleman's station and public identity. If this style seems something like Augustine's use of the Psalms to express himself, it has the opposite effect. Sutpen's rhetoric depersonalizes him, allows him to talk about himself as though he were talking about someone else, and it suggests that he does not conceive of his identity in anything like ontological terms. Moreover, he does not even conceive of himself in terms of his immediate community because he does not admit to his need for Compson's personal audience. Sutpen does not address himself to the General, but "to circum-

5. In *William Faulkner: The Yoknapatawpha Country* (New Haven, Conn.: Yale University Press, 1963), Cleanth Brooks discusses Sutpen's relation to the Jefferson community throughout his chapter on the novel. Brooks's argument is challenged by Melvin Blackman, *Faulkner: The Major Years* (Bloomington: Indiana University Press, 1966), in his chapter on *Absalom, Absalom!* A different and more germane treatment of the nature of community is to be found in Donald M. Kartiganer, "Process and Product: A Study of Modern Literary Form," Pt. 2, *Massachusetts Review*, XII (Autumn, 1971). See 806–808.

stance, to fate itself." He no longer treats his design as a personal choice or vision; he sees it as a destiny or secular providence, an obligation to the social institution he converted to as an adolescent. "Whether it was a good or a bad design is beside the point," he says. But since he has "arrived at a result absolutely and forever incredible," the role he defines for himself in making his confession lies in discovering the mistake he has made in realizing the design.[6] Because he would no more question the design than Augustine would question grace, he naturally assumes Compson's sympathy.

The immediate effect of his confession is probably not what Sutpen thinks it is going to be, for there is no way Compson can merely accept the story as, say, Wash Jones would. The ellipses and transitions are too astounding and, at one point, Compson is outraged by Sutpen's moral blindness and the impersonality he later calls "innocence."[7] Unlike Sutpen's performance, Compson's response is personal, and what it demonstrates is the power that almost any kind of intimacy can have. Although Compson cannot accept Sutpen's behavior, he can see his unadmitted need, and this understanding gives Sutpen's impulse to confess an attitude that he cannot willingly impart to his confession. Yet because Sutpen is so compelling and because his moral intelligence is so atrophied, Compson cannot remain indifferent. For his own satisfaction, he must retell Sutpen's story and develop his theory of Sutpen's innocence in an attempt to explain what Sutpen does not.

The General's own audience is surely Mr. Compson, who then transmits the story to Quentin. Exactly how the General tells his story is not developed, but it probably resembles the way in which Mr. Compson tells his. Fathers do not confess to their sons the matters of local history; they simply pass the history on in front porch conversations that have a confessional intimacy. For all the Compsons Sutpen is extremely important and through them he is frequently heard within the quotation marks of direct address. This constitutes an unusual feat of collective total recall, which

6. Faulkner, *Absalom, Absalom!*, 247, 273, 263.
7. *Ibid.*, 265.

spans at least fifty, and sometimes eighty, years. Yet Faulkner, who often seems to narrate his own parts as a participating witness rather than as the author of these events, never slights the authority of these quotations. In fact, it is the Compsons' familiarity with Sutpen that sets Quentin up for his audience with Rosa and eventually compels him to make his confession to Shreve.

Rosa knows that Quentin is the grandson of Sutpen's only confidant, and, a poetess herself, she seems to think Quentin will pursue a literary career in the North. Therefore, Quentin thinks at first that she wants to set him straight on the South's one great story. "It's because she wants it told," he says to himself. But he realizes immediately that this is not Rosa's motive for summoning him. She is much less interested in having it told than in telling it herself, for her own vindication. Although she claims to be explaining Sutpen's evil and disavows any interest in pleading her own case, she is clearly seeking from Quentin the recognition and sympathy she has never had, even from her own family. Unloved by her father, made to feel guilty for her mother's death, and raised by a crazy aunt in what Mr. Compson calls "a grim mausoleum air of Puritan righteousness and outraged female vindictiveness," Rosa has always been an isolated outsider, an aunt younger than her niece and nephew. She too thinks of Sutpen as a representative man, but not quite as the Compsons do. To Rosa he is a "fatality and curse on the South and on our family," but the real basis of her fury is Sutpen's personal indifference to her.[8]

In presenting the conventional wisdom about her enduring maidenhood, Rosa casts herself in the third person: "And that's what she cant forgive him for: not for the insult, not even for having jilted her: but for being dead." Then, as she tries to discount this explanation, she erects an astounding paraphrase that does more than confirm it.

> But I forgave him. They will tell you different, but I did. Why shouldn't I? I had nothing to forgive; I had not

8. *Ibid.*, 11, 19, 60, 21. Kartiganer, in "Process and Product," 802–803, 810–15, discusses Rosa's need for love and a sensual life, and he defines the love developed between Quentin and Shreve.

> lost him because I never owned him: a certain segment of rotten mud walked into my life, spoke that to me which I had never heard before and never shall again, and then walked out; that was all. I never owned him. . . . That did not matter. That was not even the nub of the insult. I mean that he was not owned by anyone or anything in this world, had never been, would never be, not even by Ellen, not even by Jones' granddaughter. Because he was not articulated in this world. He was a walking shadow. He was the light-blinded bat-like image of his own torment cast by the fierce demoniac lantern up from beneath the earth's crust and hence in retrograde, reverse . . . clinging, trying to cling with vain unsubstantial hands to what he hoped would hold him, save him, arrest him.

In articulating Sutpen, Rosa tries to take imaginative possession of him, to cling with her own hands to what she had hoped would hold and save her, for marriage to Sutpen would have brought her into a social and physical life she never had. Now after "the death of hope and love, the death of pride and principle, and then the death of everything save the old outraged and aghast unbelieving which has lasted for forty-three years," she "demonizes" him to justify herself and to win from Quentin an affirmation of her own identity.[9] Quentin's accompanying her out to Sutpen's to see Henry seems incidental. What Rosa needs even more is the kind of recognition from Compson's grandson that Compson gave to Sutpen himself.

Rosa's deepest needs for acceptance and love arise from an early guilt that resembles Rousseau's; her style of confession resembles the Underground Man's. Her confession contains a great deal of the social criticism that the alienated individual can direct at the society that excludes her. There is more of this criticism in Shreve's apology for Bon; but in Rosa's confession, it has the intensity of her own need. Like Dostoevsky's narrator, Rosa is too alone, self-conscious, and pathologically dependent on the com-

9. Faulkner, *Absalom, Absalom!*, 170, 171, 168.

pensation of imaginative roles. Both of them seem to approach the kind of madness that has a prophetic aspect and is generated by outrage at an extremely rigid social order. Both of them also are possessed by the disembodied imagination that substitutes rhetoric for experience and ends in virtual solipsism. Whereas Sutpen's impersonality and presumption lead him to explain too little of himself (and preserve in him the kind of self-absorption that makes Jim mysterious to Marlow), Rosa's isolation and vindictiveness compel her to explain too much.

In Chapter 5, as she tries to tell of her passage up the stairs to Judith's room, Rosa must recapitulate the story of her whole life, which is perfectly figured here in the obsessive image of her exclusion by Clytie.[10] Rosa cannot stop recounting and reinterpreting because she has nothing to rely on but her own performance and nothing to validate that performance but the response of her audience. Inevitably, however, she is also too absorbed in herself to notice Quentin's reaction—he has stopped listening. Only when he fastens on the image of Henry facing Judith across the wedding dress and begins to ask his own questions, is Rosa diverted and the chapter brought to a stop.

Quentin's fixation on Henry's incestuous love for Judith is his personal access to the Sutpen legend, and it determines his point of view later on. (It is important to remark here that Quentin is not yet concerned about Henry's relation to Bon.) In light of his family's ties to Sutpen and his encounter with Rosa, it is not surprising that Quentin returns to his father, in Chapter 2, for more information. Of more significance is his choice of Shreve as his confessor. Alienated even before he listens to Rosa, Quentin has nothing to say to anyone in Jefferson.[11] Rosa would not listen to him, since she has no room for any interpretation of Sutpen but her own; and his father does not share Quentin's emotional dis-

10. William R. Poirier, " 'Strange Gods' in Jefferson, Mississippi: Analysis of *Absalom, Absalom!*" in Frederick J. Hoffman and Olga W. Vickery (eds.), *William Faulkner: Two Decades of Criticism* (East Lansing: Michigan State College Press, 1951), 232.

11. Faulkner, *Absalom, Absalom!*, 9.

location. At Harvard, however, Quentin is something of an outsider himself, and what he has to say about Sutpen is a great deal more than merely local history. He needs an audience like Shreve precisely because another outsider gives him the necessary freedom. Quentin does not want the social acceptance Sutpen seeks from General Compson, or the intensely personal affirmation Rosa seeks from him. He has, in effect, heard both their confessions, and for himself he wants something purer. His is the only confession in the book that recognizes the confessor's value, that gives the confessor his own identity and the opportunity to make a response. Since Quentin's story calls for exactly the kind of participation it evokes from Shreve, Shreve becomes the novel's best audience and answers in kind to its most humane confession.

As Shreve enters the novel in Chapter 6, Quentin is sitting with the letter from his father, and Shreve asks a flippant question. After Quentin's minimal answer, Shreve begins to recapitulate what he knows of Rosa and the Sutpens. Obviously, there have been previous sessions; Shreve is already so familiar with the story that Quentin thinks, "He sounds just like Father."[12] Exactly how much Shreve knows at this point is a moot question, but it can be assumed that he knows the material of the first five chapters pretty much as the reader does. Before he can assume the narrative on his own, however, he still has to undergo more preparation. His purchase on the story will be Charles Bon, a point of view complementary to Quentin's affinity with Henry. Both Shreve and Bon are young foreigners who encounter the Sutpens through a college association and become interested in Sutpen's paternal responsibilities. As Shreve assumes his narrator's role, he brings Bon into focus and develops Bon's tragic quest for his father's recognition.

Shreve's preparation is his long collaborative dialogue with Quentin through Chapters 6 and 7. At first, Shreve apparently rehashes as Quentin thinks in italics. Together they fill the story in and out, backward and forward, developing the details of Wash

12. *Ibid.*, 181.

and Milly Jones and Bon's wife, son, and grandson (all of whom are outsiders fatally involved in Sutpen's design). Quentin has total recall of conversations with his father and, in Chapter 7, of his grandfather's conversations with Sutpen. Although Quentin and Shreve sound to each other like Mr. Compson, to the reader everyone sounds alike. A nice discrimination can keep the voices separate, but Faulkner creates the medley of voices deliberately.[13] As Quentin assimilates his father and grandfather, Shreve assimilates them all, and he grows to share their concern. Listening to Quentin brings Shreve further inside, so that he can eventually take his own place. Faulkner will come to call this extraordinary process "overpassing" and will define it as the condition of Shreve's community and participation with Quentin.

> All that had gone before just so much that had to be overpassed and none else present to overpass it but them, as someone always has to rake the leaves up before you can have the bonfire. That was why it did not matter to either of them which one did the talking, since it was not the talking alone which did it, performed and accomplished the overpassing, but some happy marriage of speaking and hearing wherein each before the demand, the requirement, forgave condoned and forgot the faulting of the other—faultings both in the creating of this shade whom they discussed (rather, existed in) and in the hearing and sifting and discarding the false and conserving what seemed true, or fit the preconceived—in order to overpass to love, where there might be paradox and inconsistency but nothing fault nor false.[14]

13. Vickery says, in *The Novels of William Faulkner*, 86: "Whoever the speaker, the long sentences bristle with qualifications and alternatives beneath which the syntax is lost. And what is true of the sentence is also true of the paragraph, of the chapter, indeed of the total structure. Hence the style is more closely related to the creation of the legend of Sutpen and to the common effort to fix reality and formulate truth than it is to the characters who retell the story."

14. Faulkner, *Absalom, Absalom!*, 316.

The community that overpassing creates sounds a great deal like the community Augustine describes, in which charity and joy make "but one out of many"; and what distinguishes both these communities is their openness. Part of the openness here derives from Faulkner's own attitude of participation. But the openness is essentially the issue of the love Quentin and Shreve share, which encompasses "paradox and inconsistency but nothing fault nor false." Their community does not have the rigidity of the other moral and political orders *Absalom, Absalom!* examines. Moreover, within this community, Shreve and Quentin share a power and a freedom that no other narrator in the novel experiences, for they never complain of the impotence of language that Mr. Compson, Rosa, and the General all feel as they try to explain Sutpen.[15] Their primary goal is to understand Sutpen rather than explain him, and so they overpass even the kind of aesthetic resolution that Mr. Compson would like, and that Nick cannot resist in *The Great Gatsby*. Quentin and Shreve's openness, which is both moral and aesthetic, leads them to include Charles Bon as a central figure in their account of a society that kept Bon excluded. This point of overpassing is, perhaps, *the* crucial point in *Absalom, Absalom!*—not only the epitome of its use of the confessional method, but the definition of its confessional end and ideal.

Getting to this point of overpassing, however, involves a different experience for each of the roommates. Quentin defines what happens to him when he says to himself: "But you were not listening, because you knew it already, had learned, absorbed it already without the medium of speech somehow from having been born and living beside it, with it, as children will and do: so that what your father was saying did not tell you anything so much as it struck, word by word, the resonant strings of remembering." Quentin's intuition here has the qualities of both prescience and *deja vu*, as though Sutpen were a Jungian archetype being realized in his consciousness. (The statement also explains why talking to his father has for Quentin a limited value.) It is in this state of

15. *Ibid.*, 100–101, 161, 251.

mind that Quentin begins the long account of Sutpen's life that Sutpen gave to General Compson. This is the heart of Quentin's confession, the most thorough and explicit effort to come to terms with Sutpen as he defined himself, and the most compassionate portrait of Sutpen in the novel. Coming from Quentin, after Rosa's virulence and his father's theories and bewilderment, it is especially impressive for its sympathy and justice. Shreve, who has previously interrupted with flip and incredulous questions, is noticeably silent here. When he does interrupt, it is to acknowledge his own understanding, encourage Quentin, or hasten the story on.[16] Or it is to react, as General Compson did, to the elisions and abrupt conclusions of Sutpen's original confession.

As Quentin comes to see that Shreve is reenacting his grandfather's role, he can explain to himself the continuity that is being created by this series of confessions and the way in which Shreve's capacity to participate is being made by the confessional process.

> Maybe we are both Father. Maybe nothing ever happens once and is finished. Maybe happen is never once but like ripples maybe on water after the pebble sinks, the ripples moving on, spreading, the pool attached by a narrow umbilical water-cord to the next pool which the first pool feeds, has fed, did feed, let this second pool contain a different temperature of water, a different molecularity of having seen, felt, remembered. . . .
> Yes, we are both Father. Or maybe Father and I are both Shreve, maybe it took Father and me both to make Shreve or Shreve and me both to make Father or maybe Thomas Sutpen to make all of us.

Throughout the rest of Chapter 7, Quentin's insight is borne out by the nature of Shreve's subsequent interruptions. After Quentin's important statement that Bon may not have known Sutpen was his father, Shreve breaks in to define Quentin's special authority. And twice more Shreve interrupts to take over the narrative, feeling he is ready now to extend and complete it. As this second

16. *Ibid.*, 212–13, and, for instance, 247, 258.

interruption, Quentin again testifies to Shreve's competence: "Wait, I tell you! . . . Am I going to have to hear it all again. . . . I am going to have to hear it all over again. . . . I am listening."[17] When Quentin ends his account, Shreve's preparation ends too. He has been made by Sutpen and the Compsons and by his sympathy for Charles Bon. Others have told Bon's story, but no one has given it the central importance that Shreve does.

To Mr. Compson, who does not know Bon is black and Sutpen's son, Bon is a peripheral figure and quite mysterious. "He is the curious one to me . . . seems to have withdrawn into a mere spectator, passive, a little sardonic, and completely enigmatic." This sounds a bit like Mr. Compson himself and indicates how distant from Bon his sympathies are. He can only see Bon from the outside, for he is more intrigued by Henry's problems, his vaguely homosexual attachment to Bon, the decadent rite of passage to New Orleans, and the sociology of the octoroon. Mr. Compson thinks Bon, as Judith's fiance, is a construct of the Sutpens. "Yes, shadowy: a myth, a phantom: something which they engendered and created whole themselves; some effluvium of Sutpen blood and character, as though as a man he did not exist at all."[18] All the irony in this statement is unintentional, and it is left to Shreve and Quentin to show that although Bon is literally "of Sutpen blood and character," he does not exist at all for his father because he is black.

Rosa's response to Bon is much more personal and fantastic, for she loves Bon in a way that she will later love Sutpen. Since Rosa is not close to Ellen, her access to the Sutpen family is through Judith, for whom she makes a trousseau and through whom she experiences what Mr. Compson calls "her own vicarious bridal." Rosa's own explanation in Chapter 5 is that she loved Bon, whom she never saw, not so much because of Judith but "because I who had learned nothing of love, not even parents' love—that fond dear constant violation of privacy, that stultifi-

17. *Ibid.*, 261–62, 269, 277.
18. *Ibid.*, 93, 104.

cation of the burgeoning and incorrigible I which is the meed and due of all mammalian meat, became not mistress, not beloved, but more than even love; I became all polymath love's androgynous advocate."[19] Bon became for her an imaginary abstraction —"Charles Bon, Charles Good, Charles Husband-soon-to-be."

For Shreve, these portraits of Bon are both a motive and an opportunity to respond to him with full sympathy and to provide the most moving and coherent account of the character Sutpen will not recognize, Mr. Compson does not understand, and Rosa never sees. Since Bon is never given a chance to make a full personal history of his own, even to Henry, Shreve creates one for him here.[20] And in the community that Shreve and Quentin share, Bon has a place he never had in his own life, for the two of them provide him with what they have just given to Sutpen—a family, a history, and an identity that they accept on its own terms. Shreve begins by overpassing his resemblance to Mr. Compson, for he denies Mr. Compson's hypothesis and picks up on Quentin's suggestion that Bon did not know Sutpen was his father. To explain Bon's behavior, therefore, Shreve invents a childhood for him and the story of the lawyer whose scheme is a parody of Sutpen's design. Shreve attributes Bon's longing to the fact that he realizes he is a creation of his mother and the lawyer. This invention "corrects" Mr. Compson's statement that Bon was the creation of the Sutpens' desire for an older brother, a fiance, and a son-in-law.

The lawyer episode is a good example of Shreve's style of narration, for both the tone and the material of the episode are unlike anything else in the novel.[21] Whereas Quentin's tone is "sullen" and "flat," Shreve's is exuberant and impious. The be-

19. *Ibid.*, 146.

20. The one time we certainly hear Bon himself is in his letter to Judith. A good discussion of this letter is in David L. Minter, *The Interpreted Design* (New Haven, Conn.: Yale University Press, 1969), 210–11.

21. For another discussion of Shreve's particular style, see Lynn G. Levins, "The Four Narrative Perspectives in Faulkner's *Absalom, Absalom!*," *Publications of the Modern Language Association* LXXXV (January, 1970), 35–47.

ginning of his story is filled with parentheses of qualification, new insights, and newly invented "facts." He delights, as Quentin never does, in his own powers of discovery and in the sordidness of the details he concocts: "He could go to his mother and hold the lawyer's feet to the fire anytime, like the millionaire horse has only to come in one time with a little extra sweat on him, and tomorrow he will have a new jock. Sure, that's who it would be: the lawyer, that lawyer with his private mad female millionaire to farm."[22] The spontaneity of this passage is indicative of the quality of Shreve's whole narrative. Later Shreve's style will acquire a more sober urgency, but it will never lose the sense of self-conscious fictionalizing that Faulkner recognizes as one of the necessary effects of overpassing.

Faulkner makes his explanation of overpassing immediately before Shreve announces to Quentin, "And now . . . we are going to talk about love." Quentin seems to expect him to talk about Bon and Judith as his father and Rosa have, for Quentin himself is still puzzling the facts that concern Henry's feelings toward the couple. But Shreve is on his own momentum, and the love he begins to talk about is Bon's love for Sutpen and his need for his father's recognition. Shreve takes the relationship with Judith as given, fatal, and sees Bon pursuing it as the means to another end. When Quentin objects, "But its not love," Shreve insists it is and goes on describing the lawyer's letter to Henry and Bon's growing intuition about the letter, which inspires him to use Henry to get to Sutpen. As Shreve tightens and accelerates this plot, he creates a pathos for Bon, which no one else has seen in him, as he waits for word from his father. Shreve says on Bon's behalf: "Maybe he will write it then. He would just have to write 'I am your father. Burn this' and I would do it. Or if not that, a sheet, a scrap of paper with the one word 'Charles' in his hand, and I would know what he meant and he would not even have to ask me to burn it. Or a lock of his hair or a paring from his finger nail and I would know them because I believe now that I have

22. Faulkner, *Absalom, Absalom!*, 255, 300.

known what his hair and his finger nails would look like all my life, could choose that lock and that paring out of a thousand." Shreve has Bon willing to renounce Judith, if that is what Sutpen wants; and simply acknowledged by his father, Bon would then ride off without asking for any explanation or apology.[23]

Shreve has to keep altering his story as he sees more acutely into Bon's pain. "Think of his heart then," Shreve says twice, and he recasts the relationship between Bon and Henry as they spend the war together hoping that time itself will resolve their problem. Henry's problem at this point is incest, and he begins to look for precedents. Shreve also alters Mr. Compson's account of the wound at Shiloh, maintaining that it is actually Bon who rescues Henry even after proposing that Henry "accidentally" shoot him in battle. This theme of fraternal love, more dignified and compelling than Mr. Compson's suspicions of homosexuality, is brought to its conclusion when Henry and Bon confront each other after Henry has just spoken to his father in the tent in Carolina. The problem is no longer merely incest, but miscegenation; and Bon, desperate for his father's recognition, tells Henry he will have to shoot him in order to stop him from returning to marry Judith. "Henry looks at the pistol; now he is not only panting, he is trembling; when he speaks now his voice is not even the exhalation, it is the suffused and suffocating inbreath itself:—You are my brother.—No I'm not. I'm the nigger that's going to sleep with your sister. Unless you stop me, Henry."[24]

While Shreve's imaginative participation complements Quentin's natural debt to the facts, it also liberates Quentin to use his own imagination in discovering a more fitting truth about Bon's behavior and motives. Bon cannot back out; but it is not his defiance of Sutpen that brings about his death, it is his need for a father. In the other narrators' accounts, Henry simply murders Bon; in Quentin and Shreve's, Bon cooperates in his own death and gives it the character of a romantic suicide. In giving Bon the full humanity that the South and the Sutpen family never allowed

23. *Ibid.*, 316–18, 326, 327.
24. *Ibid.*, 329, 330, 357–58.

him, Shreve gives him as well a perfect final gesture of compassion towards Judith: he leaves in the metal case Judith has given him, not her picture, but a picture of his octoroon wife and his son. Shreve says: "Don't you know? It was because he said to himself, 'If Henry dont mean what he said, it will be all right; I can take it out and destroy it. But if he does mean what he said, it will be the only way I will have to say to her, *I was no good: do not grieve for me.*' Aint that right? Aint it? By God, aint it?" Quentin answers yes.[25] Judith, who loves Bon too, seems to have understood the gesture perfectly.

With Bon's death, Shreve can do no more, and he begins disengaging himself with his remarks about the difference between his background and Quentin's. In the last chapter of the novel, which is really Quentin's alone, he remembers his trip with Rosa to see Henry. Shreve handles some of the narration, but what he says is simply a reiteration of the story Quentin has told him sometime before. The community they have shared no longer holds because Quentin cannot "hate the South" and reverts to it as Henry Sutpen did; Shreve now has no more to say than Bon had. Quentin and Shreve cannot overpass the fact that Bon is dead, killed in effect by the hubris and exclusivity that Sutpen assumed when he first confided in General Compson. But in responding with such extraordinary sympathy, Shreve has fulfilled the immediate hope with which any confession is made; and then by overpassing to love, he has allowed Quentin to define himself in a way that has also allowed both Sutpen and Bon their full identities too and Bon a place, at least for a moment, where "niggers" can be loved as brothers.

Quentin's pain and loneliness on the novel's final page are ineluctable, however, for Faulkner sees no honest escape from the weight of history. The community created by overpassing can embody a counterideal to the society embodied in Sutpen, but it cannot repair all the sins of the fathers. Even with Shreve's participation, the confessional form of *Absalom, Absalom!* remains

25. *Ibid.*, 359.

open, containing paradox and inconsistency, but is no more capable of resolving them than of resolving a human's identity. Yet the power of the novel grows from Faulkner's great effort to find a form that does acknowledge the individual's primary value and at the same time tries to achieve the kind of community individuals need for their confirmation. *Absalom, Absalom!*'s development of the confession seems to be the culmination of Faulkner's long experiment with the narrative techniques he used to explore the tragic isolation of the Compsons in *The Sound and the Fury* and the Bundrens in *As I Lay Dying*, both of which are novels, like *Absalom, Absalom!*, intensely concerned with the tensions between individuality and community within a family. David Minter has suggested that the tension between individuality and community in *Light in August* is even stronger, for that novel's two main characters, Lena Grove and Joe Christmas, do not even meet.[26] The various voices that narrate *Light in August* are not conscious of one another, and the only union that is anything like Quentin and Shreve's is the union between Byron Bunch and Gail Hightower, who can talk to each other because they exist outside the community that executes Joe Christmas. But their conversation is not confessional in the strictest sense, and its intimacy is not so certainly efficacious as the intimacy shared by the furniture dealer and his wife in the last chapter. They have a "happy marriage of speaking and hearing" literally realized in a marriage bed.

The success of Faulkner's method in *Absalom, Absalom!* did not guarantee the success of the similar method he employs in his later novel *The Town*. In *The Town* a chorus of narrators are again concerned with the life and upward mobility of the novel's central figure. But neither Flem Snopes's character nor his career demands the kind of attention given to Sutpen. The speakers of *The Town* are alert to Flem but never obsessed by him, and their encounter with the Snopes phenomenon is closer to sociology

26. David L. Minter, Introduction, in David L. Minter (ed.), *Light in August: A Collection of Critical Essays* (Englewood Cliffs, N.J.: Prentice-Hall, 1969), 6.

than it is to the mythologizing, the romance, the confession and apology that inform *Absalom, Absalom!* Flem, despite his malevolence, is never the threat to Gavin Stevens that Sutpen is to Rosa and even to General Compson. To Ratliff, Flem is never the embodiment of a great historical process in the way that Sutpen is to Mr. Compson. The difference between the two novels is even more apparent in the difference between the young narrators. Like Quentin, Chick Mallison undergoes an education, and he is initiated into his role in the novel by the conversation and instruction of the other narrators. But Chick never engages Flem, never confronts the meaning of Flem's life and its relation to his own, in the way Quentin engages Sutpen or Shreve engages Bon. And when Chick begins to sound like Gavin, it is clearly a weakness in the organization of the novel's points of view. It does not reflect the deliberate strategy Faulkner uses in *Absalom, Absalom!* to prepare for the independence Quentin and Shreve exercise in creating the story of Sutpen's real relation to Bon.

The Town, in other words, is not informed by confession, because confession itself involves more than conversation. It begins in self-identification and ends in community, which is necessarily open and therefore open to the reader's participation. Faulkner himself has acknowledged the reader's role in the meaning of *Absalom, Absalom!* He has said that if the narrators represent "all these thirteen ways of looking at the blackbird, the reader has his own fourteenth image of the blackbird which I would like to think is the truth."[27] But this response oversimplifies, I think, what *Absalom, Absalom!* and Faulkner's technique suggest the truth to be: not a single, synthetic "fourteenth" image, but "some happy marriage of speaking and hearing" that continues the confessional process and remains necessarily unresolved. If the reader's self-conscious entailment is the "end" of any open-ended fiction, if he is the outer circle of the community a confession creates, his response is also another beginning. The sympathetic reader who sub-

27. William Faulkner, *Faulkner in the University*, ed. Frederick L. Gwynn and Joseph L. Blottner (Charlottesville: University of Virginia Press, 1959), 274.

mits himself to the process of confession and who reenacts in his own way the roles of General Compson, Quentin, and Shreve, renews the novel's enterprise, confirms its speakers and their difficult search for freedom and love, and extends its community. And it is clearly the design of Faulkner's confessional procedures to "make" the reader in much the same way that Shreve has been made, to lead the reader to see Shreve as a model.

To accept Shreve as our model means acknowledging unattractive qualities in ourselves. Shreve is initially callous toward Quentin's pain in the way young men can be callous to each other out of self-defense; his aggressiveness and incredulity lead him to taunt Quentin; and his final question about why Quentin hates the South seems, at the moment, simple and cruel. Shreve is, like Marlow's privileged man, the kind of confessor Quentin needs and also a natural antagonist. Yet Shreve is allowed to answer Quentin, and the imagination Faulkner bestows on Shreve makes him the freest character in the novel. Quentin's muted confession is something like Sutpen's. Quentin has nothing of Sutpen's blind arrogance, and he is a victim of "the design" in a different way, but he is unusually reticent about himself. This passivity, Quentin's honorable impersonality and refusal to rage, contribute to our sense that Shreve seems too cool, less compassionate than he should be. Nonetheless, Shreve's response is a great deal more than General Compson's. Shreve sees Bon and Bon's pain; he sees more in the story than the way the story has been told; and in this sense, he is a good confessor despite his limitations.

Moreover, insofar as the confessors in these four novels—Jephson, Nick, Marlow, and Quentin—are also figures of the artist, Shreve is quite remarkable. His skepticism is cleaner than Marlow's because he has nothing personally at stake in Sutpen's or Quentin's history. In the place of the privileged man, we want to stand up for Marlow and answer his questions immediately. Because of Shreve, however, we can respond to *Absalom, Absalom!* without confessing ourselves, without apologizing in our turn for Shreve, because Faulkner has opened up the confessional form so widely. When we do respond to all we have heard from all the

Chapter 8

"Approaching Carolina"

Most serious thought in our time struggles with the feeling of homelessness. The felt unreliability of human experience brought out by the inhuman acceleration of historical change has led every sensitive modern mind to the recording of some kind of nausea, of intellectual vertigo. And the only way to cure this spiritual nausea seems to be, at least initially, to exacerbate it. Modern thought is pledged to a kind of applied Hegelianism: seeking its Self in its Other. Europe seeks itself in the exotic—in Asia, in the Middle East, among pre-literate peoples, in a mythic America; a fatigued rationality seeks itself in the impersonal energies of sexual ecstasy or drugs; consciousness seeks its meaning in unconsciousness; humanistic problems seek their oblivion in scientific "value neutrality" and quantification. The "other" is experienced as a harsh purification of the "self."

SUSAN SONTAG
Against Interpretation

There is nothing final to say about confession. The definition I have proposed in this essay—confession is the deliberate, self-conscious attempt of an individual to identify himself, to explain his nature to the audience who represents the kind of community he needs to exist in and confirm him—makes confession a formal relationship between the speaker and the confessor, in life as well as in literature. Novels as different as *Moll Flanders* and *Absalom, Absalom!* suggest that this definition of confession does not depend on any particular notion of human nature or character; it does not assume that all confessional novels will fill a prescription; and it does not point toward a specific social or political goal in the notion of community. Community is as open an idea as the notion of the self. It is the warmly persuasive word that designates a positive alternative to the speaker's condition, a better quality of human relationship that he hopes will resolve the situation which motivates his confession and will give his life a meaning beyond himself. There is nothing final to say about confession because the situation of the individual speaker will always determine his choice of a confessor, the themes he develops in his confession, the benefits he wants from their relationship, and the shape of the novel his confession may inform. Confession, as it appears in the novel, by its very nature resists more generalization than this with the same energy any individual confession resists becoming mere literature.

Because of this resistance, the novels we have considered here are a fair sample of the range of the confessional form. They are, of course, an arbitrary order, but the standing of each keeps the order from being personally eccentric; and while they do not exhaust every possibility a confessional novel may realize, they do not too neatly delimit the conclusions we can draw. In fact, these novels suggest two completely different conclusions about the confession's apparent development or possible growth. The first conclusion derives from what we can call the argument according to art, the second from the argument according to life. The argument from art suggests that recent ideas about the self, and the complex uses the confessional form has already been put to, should make a confession very difficult for anyone who is not an accomplished writer. The argument from life suggests that the meaning and success of a confession lie in its reception rather than its expression, with the audience rather than the speaker, so that naïve expression can be rescued from its own artlessness without any essential loss.

The argument according to art we can epitomize in the examples of *Notes from Underground* and *Moby-Dick,* which, because of their prophetic awareness of the human unconscious and modern problems of knowledge, seem to cancel forever the chance of another confessional novel as unself-conscious and unironic as *Moll Flanders.* Even *An American Tragedy,* which resists aesthetic resolutions emphatically, is still a more artful structure than Dreiser's prose style makes it seem. And subsequent ideas about the self that have sponsored wholly unanticipated disciplines, like psychiatry and cognitive anthropology, have exerted an even greater pressure on literature to find new styles adequate to concepts of the self that question the very idea of individuality and the validity of personal experience.[1]

Jean Paul Sartre and John Barth, for instance, are writers for whom the self seems to be little more than the always inadequate conventions the self has for its own expression. In *The Words,* Sartre in effect denies the very project of confession by repudiating the idea that the individual finds his identity in community, and he does this by attacking his own need as a young child to define himself in the eyes and expectations of his family. He later achieves some independence of them by adapting roles for himself from adventure literature, but he apparently continues to write in order to realize the state of authenticity, outside of time and convention, that is either reification or death. *The Words,* which is a thug's title for the autobiography of a writer, makes almost no mention of Sartre's great public career or his life of work, and its own ruthless integrity gives Sartre a posture not very different from Rousseau's.

There are no similar postures in Barth's fictions in *Lost in the Funhouse,* for there is a despair about them that comes from his

1. Susan Sontag's essays contain primary statements of some of these ideas against the traditional ideas of the self. See her *Against Interpretation* (New York: Dell, 1967).

reduction of all self-expression and autobiography itself to, well, words. "Autobiography" is a story about itself, told in "its own words," that begins, "You who listen give me life in a manner of speaking."[2] This mixture of imperative and invitation is not unlike the tone Ishmael develops in some of his most characteristic passages, and the sharp curve at the end of the sentence sounds like a trick of the Underground Man's. Barth's opening line is both a paradigm and a parody of confessional address that reveals all of the dependency, all of what Sartre would call the bad faith, all of the substancelessness of the motto from Novalis that Conrad uses to explain the heart of the confessions in *Lord Jim* ("It is certain my conviction gains infinitely, the moment another soul will believe in it"). Barth's line even reduces that other soul, the "you who" listens, to the pun yoo-hoo.

These examples of minimalism, which have counterparts in the novels of Samuel Beckett and Alain Robbe-Grillet, are balanced but not canceled by the writers who deny the traditional products of self-expression for the reason that the self is so irreducibly multiple it cannot be contained in the old jars. Virginia Woolf's *Orlando*, for instance, is a novel that attacks the enterprise of historical biography and its idea of articulate identity simply by allowing its subject to live for over three hundred years as both a man and a woman, to be by turns both father and mother, and to be never older than thirty-six. *Orlando* is a comic embodiment of Woolf's ideas about androgyny and time; and although Orlando herself finally completes the poem begun when she was a Renaissance youth, it is never suggested that "The Oak Tree" expresses Orlando as comprehensively as Woolf's authorial omniscience can. It would be difficult, it would require a much longer novel, for

2. John Barth, "Autobiography," in *Lost in the Funhouse* (New York: Bantam Books, 1969), 33. Barth's essay "The Literature of Exhaustion" is also relevant here. It is reprinted in Marcus Klein (ed.), *The American Novel Since World War II* (New York: Fawcett Publications, 1969), 267–279. And Barth's character Henry Burlingame, in *The Sot-Weed Factor*, is as dazzling an example of the other side of this argument, the character of multiple identities, as there is in American fiction.

Orlando to show us what Woolf can tell us about her quite quickly.

> Then she called hesitatingly, as if the person she wanted might not be there, "Orlando?" For if there are (at a venture) seventy-six different times all ticking in the mind at once, how many different people are there not— Heaven help us— all having lodgment at one time or another in the human spirit? Some say two thousand and fifty-two. So that it is the most usual thing in the world for a person to say, directly they are alone, Orlando? (if that is one's name) meaning by that Come, come! I'm sick to death of this particular self. I want another. Hence, the astonishing changes we see in our friends. But it is not altogether plain sailing, either, for though one may say, as Orlando said (being out in the country and needing another self presumably) Orlando? still the Orlando she needs may not come; these selves of which we are built up, one on top of another, as plates are piled on a waiter's hand, have attachments elsewhere, sympathies, little constitutions and rights of their own, call them what you will (and for many of these things there is no name) so that one will only come if it is raining, another in a room with green curtains, another when Mrs. Jones is not there, another if you can promise it a glass of wine—and so on; for everybody can multiply from his own experience the different terms which his different selves have made with him— and some are too wildly ridiculous to be mentioned in print at all.[3]

Ideas of the self like Woolf's or Joyce's, and now Pynchon's, have made omniscient, even encyclopedic narrators essential to the modernist novel that wants to explore the fullness of human

3. Virginia Woolf, *Orlando: A Biography* (New York: Harcourt Brace Jovanovich, 1956), 308–309.

identity; and the writers who want nonetheless to test the limits of self-expression have often been forced into using multiple points of view to present the nature of character fairly. We have seen this already in Conrad and Faulkner, and we can see it under another aspect in Norman Mailer. Mailer may be an unlikely partner for Virginia Woolf, but they are not incongruent. In *Orlando* and *The Armies of the Night*, Woolf and Mailer both try to erase or redraw the line between history and fiction, and Mailer believes as firmly as Woolf that the self is legion. He seems to believe, in fact, that some of his selves are too wildly ridiculous *not* to be mentioned in print, and he begins to enumerate these selves as soon as he casts the protagonists of the memoir he pretends is a novel as "Mailer." Mailer is not simply playing both Marlow and Lord Jim, nor is he adopting an identity like Ishmael's after a symbolic rebirth. He writes of "Mailer" as though he were someone else, his own other. "It was his theory—not too novel an hypothesis—that many people who had never acted, and could never begin to act on stage without training, still had several extraordinary characterizations they could bring to a film provided they spoke their own words and had no script to remember."[4] Mailer takes a certain presumptuous pride in the dramaturgy of the speeches he delivers and in his ability to do the voices of Lyndon Johnson, a black radical, and an Irish cop. And he describes his selves as not only the Protagonist and the Novelist, the Director and the Historian, and the witness to the Beast, but after seeing himself in a television documentary he says: "For a warrior, presumptive general, ex-political candidate, embattled aging enfant terrible of the literary world, wise father of six children, radical intellectual, existential philosopher, hard working author, champion of obscenity, husband for four battling sweet wives, amiable bar drinker, and much exaggerated street fighter, party giver, hostess insulter—he had on screen in his first documentary a fatal taint, a last remain-

4. Norman Mailer, *The Armies of the Night: History as a Novel/The Novel as History* (New York: New American Library, 1968), 153–54. Note the subtitles of Woolf's and Mailer's novels.

ing speck of the one personality he found absolutely insupportable —the nice Jewish boy from Brooklyn."[5]

This sense of his own nature allows Mailer to surpass and extend himself in unexampled ways, and the principle of multiplicity obviously supplants a principle of community as the end in which an individual seeks confirmation of his identity. But Mailer also acknowledges the expense of this principle in his undisguised admiration for the integrity of Robert Lowell. Lowell is in no way the outsider Mailer still feels himself to be. Lowell is, in fact, to Mailer what Queequeg is to Ishmael—both the prince and the natural man. And obviously Mailer's dramatic public and political acts do not satisfy the need for completion he achieves in the act of writing *The Armies of the Night.* This work is different from his other journalism and better than his other novels because it not only records the history and interprets the event, it also resolves his own autobiographical impulse and his ideas of identity into a singular form.

The examples of Woolf and Mailer and the argument from art suggest that confession is now too difficult to make without considerable literary skill; or it is no longer a necessary act, because each of us is already a community within, like Quentin Compson —not an entity but a commonwealth. The argument from life, however, obviates the expressive problems that challenge Sartre and Barth, Woolf and Mailer, by giving to the confessor the responsibility for creating meaning. This principle, which arises from the fact that confession is a communicative as well as an expressive act, is stated very clearly in the confessions of Rousseau, who understood the problems of expression with great clarity and who tried, at least at the beginning of his work, to resist expressive form. Rousseau says of his reader and the reader's role:

> If I made myself responsible for the result and said to him, "Such is my character," he might suppose, if not that I am deceiving him, at least that I am deceiving

5. *Ibid.*, 153.

> myself. But by relating to him in simple detail all that has happened to me, all that I have done, all that I have felt, I cannot lead him into error, unless wilfully; and even if I wish to, I shall not easily succeed by this method. His task is to assemble these elements and to assess the being who is made up of them. The summing-up must be his, and if he comes to wrong conclusions, the fault will be his own making. But, with this in view, it is not enough for my story to be truthful, it must be detailed as well. It is not for me to judge of the relative importance of events; I must relate them all, and leave the selection to him. That is the task to which I have devoted myself up to this point with all my courage; and I shall not relax in the sequel.[6]

Although Rousseau is characteristically self-serving in this passage and ultimately violates his own intention to give the reader freedom, he does make way here for the confessors we have seen in Reuben Jephson, Nick Carraway, Marlow, Quentin, and Shreve. They represent the kind of audience who, for its own reason, is ready to redeem the inarticulate with compassion and understanding, or to make more of a book than it is in itself. Their own needs make confessions out of statements not intended to be so, and they take these statements personally because it is useful for them.

Two recent examples of this kind of audience can be found in the readership of Erica Jong's *Fear of Flying* and *The Autobiography of Malcolm X*, each of which also redraws the line between fiction and history or art and life. *Fear of Flying* was an event not so much because of Jong's literary skill as her audience. *Fear of Flying* is not even a formal confession. But its psychological and sexual intimacy, and the candid, funny language it uses to repudiate the conventions of family, marriage, and psychiatry give it the kind of immediacy of address and desire for renewal we recognize

6. *The Confessions of Jean-Jacques Rousseau*, trans. J. M. Cohen (Harmondsworth, England: Penguin Books, 1953), 169–70.

as confessional. And because Isadora Wing seems to resemble Jong herself, *Fear of Flying* has the feeling of truth that is often more important to a novel's contemporary readership than to its posterity, who are more likely to prize its formal values. It is probably misleading to say *Fear of Flying* created its audience, as a confession must do to fulfill its own intention. But it is probably not misleading to say its success and utility arose in an audience already there and ready to be identified as different from their husbands, families, lovers, and the disinterested reader.

Malcolm X's intended reader cannot be disinterested; his autobiography is a classical religious confession, which resembles both Augustine's and Moll Flanders', and which Malcolm intended to be useful, instructive, and edifying. As his story progresses, however, he explains what has happened to him in a life he has called "a chronology of—*changes*"; his intended audience grows as he alters his idea of the kind of community he belongs to.[7] When he moves from the state home in rural Michigan to the black community of Roxbury, he changes from the white folks' "mascot" into Shorty's "Homeboy" and finds a world, a culture, and an audience he could not have imagined. It is to this world, this poor, urban audience that he is always most attached; yet his conversion to the Black Muslims gives him not only a new name, but a more articulate myth and another community he could not have imagined. Then the expulsion by Elijah Muhammad that leads Malcolm to Mecca and into orthodox, international Islam gives him another new name, El-Hajj Malik El-Shabazz; an even larger community; and a still greater identity as a political leader of international stature. Malcolm never forgets that his primary audience is composed of people like his own family, but he is very conscious by the end of his autobiography to include everyone who will listen under the rubric of the "objective reader."

> I have given to this book so much of whatever time I have because I feel, and I hope, that if I honestly and

7. Malcolm X, *The Autobiography of Malcolm X* (New York: Grove Press, 1966), 339.

> fully tell my life's account, read objectively it might prove to be a testimony of some social value.
>
> I think that an objective reader may see how in the society to which I was exposed as a black youth here in America, for me to wind up in a prison was just about inevitable. It happens to so many thousands of black youth.
>
> I think that an objective reader may see how when I heard "The white man is the devil," when I played back what had been my own experiences, it was inevitable that I would respond positively; then the next twelve years of my life were devoted and dedicated to propagating that phrase among the black people.
>
> I think, I hope, that the objective reader, in following my life—the life of only one ghetto-created Negro—may gain a better picture and understanding than he has previously had of the black ghettoes which are shaping the lives and the thinking of almost all of the 22 million Negroes who live in America.
>
> . . . .
>
> In this year, 1965, I am certain that more—and worse—riots are going to erupt, in yet more cities, in spite of the conscience-saving Civil Rights Bill. The reason is that the *cause* of these riots, the racist malignancy in America, has been too long unattended.[8]

Of course, at the time of the autobiography's publication, even the "objective reader" was necessarily aware of the civil rights and antiwar movements and of the climate of violence in which Malcolm himself was assassinated, or martyred. His autobiography is a great book because Malcolm was a great man, but reading it on a campus immediately affected by the New Left was a very different experience than rereading it now, more than ten years later, in the political torpor characterized in part by the apparently imminent defeat of the Equal Rights Amendment. The university

8. *Ibid.*, 378–79.

audience that comprised so many of Malcolm's objective readers in the sixties now contains readers who are not subjective by contrast, but much more self-concerned and convinced that their reaction is prudent, healthful. And Malcolm's only successor as a political figure is apparently Muhammad Ali, who is no longer a Muslim or a militant either, but is simply empowered by an unprecedented celebrity.

A more significant and more strictly literary figure of Malcolm's confessional audience may be Alex Haley, who assisted Malcolm in the production of his book. It is important and appropriate that Malcolm did not *write* his autobiography, that he in fact even resisted writing it, for the act of writing—as we have seen in the cases of the Underground Man and Ishmael, Sartre and Mailer—always implies a private act of self-creation, a process that Malcolm underwent in prison when he regained his literacy and reformed his life himself by writing "a million words." His conversion to Islam, however, he did not think of as an act of his own will—it was the will of Allah—and his intense need to identify with a group led him always to deny his personal agency. He said, "Everything that happens — Islam teaches — is written," which meant he was to take no creative credit for his autobiography, and which therefore removed it from exclusively aesthetic judgments.[9] Malcolm, like Augustine, was a proud, powerful man who was always trying to be humble; and Alex Haley, therefore, was more than his amanuensis. He was the means by which Malcolm could produce an autobiography "impersonally," almost naïvely, and a representative of the community Malcolm ultimately had to reach and join. As a retired Coast Guardman and an educated, professional writer, Haley is the kind of black man Malcolm hated the way Mailer hates liberals. Haley, however, allowed Malcolm to deliver his confession orally, which is an appropriate mode for a charismatic black religious and political leader, and Haley's living audience obviously gave Malcolm access to the kind of response he did not expect anywhere but in the ghetto or the mosque.

9. *Ibid.*, 172, 211.

Haley's attention to Malcolm made Malcolm "one of us" in a way he could not have been by himself. And Haley's own book, *Roots*, is related to *The Autobiography of Malcolm X* in the way Nick's manuscript is related to Gatsby's confession; it is not nearly as honest, and it reaches for myth.

If we look to the speakers, to the argument according to art, confession seems increasingly difficult to make; for any confession requires unusual self-awareness and the courage to face shame, estrangement, or guilt in front of a confessor; but confession now seems also to require an aesthetic self-consciousness as well. Scholes and Kellogg's statement that "all knowing and all telling are subject to the conventions of art" is not necessarily to the advantage of the unsophisticated speaker, as we have seen in the very different cases of Moll Flanders and Clyde Griffiths. On the other hand, the argument according to life is that a confessor more competent than the speaker can hear a confession and make something of it that the speaker could not accomplish alone. A confessor who is simply different can have the same effect, as readers of different generations or gender can prefer the feminism of *Moll Flanders* now to the absurdity of *Notes from Underground*, or the racial significance of *Absalom, Absalom!* to that of *Lord Jim*. In every case, however, confession does not depend solely on the speaker and his expression, or solely on the confessor and his interpretation. Confession and the community it seeks are mutually dependent, create a relationship that can never be absolute, exist in "some happy marriage of speaking and hearing . . . where there might be paradox and inconsistency but nothing fault nor false." And out of this constant intercourse, out of the need to explain ourselves regardless of the difficulties, and our equivalent need to hear each other's explanations, confessions will always come, changing as our ideas of the self change and alter the requirements of community, but reasserting always the incontrovertible primacy of the speaker and his experience. For confession, there is, there can be, no other end.

Index